INTEGRATED

INTEGRATED

HOW
AMERICAN SCHOOLS
FAILED
BLACK CHILDREN

NOLIWE ROOKS

PANTHEON BOOKS / NEW YORK

FIRST HARDCOVER EDITION
PUBLISHED BY PANTHEON BOOKS 2025

Published by Pantheon Books, a division of Penguin Random House LLC,
1745 Broadway, New York, New York 10019.

Pantheon Books and the colophon are registered trademarks of
Penguin Random House LLC.

LCCN: 2024950436
ISBN: 978-0-553-38739-1 (hardcover)
ISBN: 978-0-553-38740-7 (ebook)

penguinrandomhouse.com | pantheonbooks.com

Printed in the United States of America

1 3 5 7 9 10 8 6 4 2

The authorized representative in the EU for product safety and
compliance is Penguin Random House Ireland, Morrison Chambers,
32 Nassau Street, Dublin D02 YH68, Ireland, https://eu-contact.penguin.ie.

For my grandparents,
Evelyn Baker Rooks and Milton Perry Rooks Sr.,
master teachers who ordered my steps, dreamed me a world,
and still inspire me to hope when my faith falters.

hope

/hōp/

noun: **hope**

a feeling of expectation and desire for a certain thing to
happen.

ruined

/'rōoind/

adjective: **ruined**

reduced to a state of decay, collapse, or disintegration;
of having been irreparably damaged or harmed.

CONTENTS

INTEGRATED

INTRODUCTION

In April 2021, a lawyer friend told me a story about one of her clients: a little girl with milk-chocolate skin who lived in the South Bronx. She loved her elementary school filled with children whose skin color ranged from the first light of dawn to the depths of midnight. Her classmates had family members on islands like Puerto Rico and the Dominican Republic, or on the closer island of Manhattan. The little girl admired her teachers, cherished her friends, and relished learning. She always, according to her mother, looked forward to school.

I heard that part just fine. It took me a minute to fully grasp the rest: One day, the little girl came home and, with squealed excitement, shared the news that her class was going on a field trip to a rich school. They would, she said, ride yellow buses, meet other children, and see different teachers. She assured her mother she would be on her "best behavior." A few days after the trip, a teacher found the little girl at her desk, scratching away at her arm with a paper clip. She was trying to erase the chocolate-hued top layer of her skin and "free" the white skin hiding underneath. She had decided that the skin, *her* skin, was the reason she didn't go to a pretty school like the one she and her classmates had visited on that field trip, and it made her feel sad.

One of the most disturbing aspects of this story, I think, is that she was not altogether wrong. School segregation has always benefited white and wealthy children who attend well-resourced, fully staffed, well-maintained schools. Meanwhile, a distressingly high number of poor, Black, Indigenous, and Latino children attend schools that are underfunded, crumbling, and understaffed. In heartbreaking fashion, this little girl showed the violent impact of the segregated educational system in the United States, using her skin to make the point. And she is neither the first nor the last child to have been exposed to this sort of educational inequity and be left broken by the experience.

This is a book about how segregation in schools in the United States has consistently been remade and reinforced to keep those at both the top and the bottom of the social caste system so firmly anchored in their positions that, despite the (admittedly sporadic and episodic) efforts to integrate schools, we have been unable to significantly dislodge this inequity. It is about how the dream of widespread integration became a tepid desegregation, wherein as small a number as possible of Black children were, like pepper on popcorn, lightly sprinkled atop wealthy, white school environments, while most others were left behind. It is about what is buried below the surface of integration efforts in the United States and what must be found, dug up, and properly laid to rest to adequately understand and address the inequalities in our present educational system.

When refracted through the prism of one truth, the movement to desegregate or share the benefits and promises of public education in the United States is a story of hope, promise, and opportunity. When refracted through the light of a different truth, it is an undertold tale about ruin and underexplored historical and contemporary trauma. The dream of one system that would serve all children equally, giving Black children access to the same educational opportunities as the wealthy, ultimately came true for only a select few. This is so even in schools with a relatively equal number of students from distinct racial and economic backgrounds. In such schools, students who are in higher-performing classrooms are rarely Black or Latino, and those in the lowest tracks are rarely white or Asian. Though they share a school building, academic and ability sorting and tracking ensure that their paths rarely actually cross. Integration as it was initially imagined has rarely happened.

Brown v. Board of Education, the landmark civil rights case that was meant to equalize education between white and Black students, was born from sustained efforts by the National Association for the Advancement of Colored People (NAACP). In 1935, NAACP lawyers began filing educational equalization lawsuits arguing that, so long as Black citizenship was not recognized as equal citizenship under the law, separate educational systems based on race were not and could never be equal: schools educating white children and wealthy children would always have more, and Black children would never gain access to the clean, well-equipped classrooms that they, too, deserved. Five different cases brought on behalf of parents across Delaware, Washington, D.C., Virginia, South Carolina, and Kansas between 1950 and 1954 called for the court to help schools better educate Black children by mandating racial integration. The five were eventually consolidated into *Brown v. Board,* bundled together to strengthen the argument about the regional, if not national, harms of segregated education.

According to weather reports, the day the Supreme Court announced its decision in the *Brown v. Board of Education* case, the world looked hazy and gray. Clouds obscured the sky, and mist hung and hovered in Topeka, Kansas, where Black and white people inside homes and businesses waited to hear how the court would rule in the case, in which the town's Board of Education was a named defendant. When word came, it was ostensibly a loss for segregation and a win for democracy. The Supreme Court decreed that mandating that Black and white children attend schools based primarily or solely on their racial or ethnic background was unconstitutional. *Brown* was meant to strike down unequal forms of citizenship and extend the surety of equal education to all, regardless of race. It was hailed by many across the nation as a significant victory for Black people, whose children had long had to endure impediments to their education—learning in poorly funded, sometimes physically unsound buildings; having school years lengthened and shortened based on the labor needs of local farmers; and having access only to outdated, worn-out textbooks and classroom furniture.

Here's the problem: much of what we know about the desires Black people had for educational integration is incomplete, or rather comprised of information learned in ellipses and fragments. In reality, not all Black parents believed *Brown v. Board* was a decision in the best interest of their children. A decade after *Brown,* Constance Baker Motley, the former NAACP Legal Defense Fund attorney who was part of the strategy team for *Brown v. Board,* wrote that she believed the organization had overestimated the extent to which Black people shared the organization's staunch opposition to segregated schools. "We didn't really get any real grass roots activity around school desegregation," she said, adding that she believed this was, in part, because schools in Black communities functioned not only as educational institutions, but also as "economic lifelines and community centers." There was an understanding among Black people that what might be gained from integration would come at a great cost. Because of this, the civil rights historian Adam Fairclough has noted, in the years leading up to *Brown,* "NAACP officials had a hard time convincing their members that integration would be more effective than [funding] equalization in obtaining a better education for their children."

From the onset, while the NAACP advanced their work toward dismantling segregation, some Black people in Topeka had organized themselves to fight *against* the NAACP and its championing of integrated schools. Theirs was a district that equally funded the education of Black and white children. Black teachers and administrators were paid the same as their white counterparts. Black children sat in school buildings as sturdy, well heated, and cooled as any school in town. Books and materials were in good shape and purchased new. Black people were proud of the education their children received and were worried they would not be well served in integrated schools. Polled in the months leading up to the ruling, 54 percent of Black people in Topeka said they preferred things as they were. They didn't see the point in ending a system that, though separate, was truly equal and working well for them and their children.

Not even those involved in *Brown v. Board* were completely aligned with the NAACP's desegregationist agenda. Leola Brown, the mother of the titular plaintiff in *Brown v. Board,* said she and her husband did not file the lawsuit because they were dissatisfied with the teachers or education their daughter Linda had received in her all-Black school. On the contrary, Brown had a lot of positive things to say about Monroe Elementary, the segregated Black school Linda attended. Speaking of the school, she said, "Oh, I loved it. I loved it. The teachers were fantastic! We got a fantastic education there. It wasn't, as I say, this case wasn't based on that because we had fantastic teachers and we learned! We learned a lot and they were good to us, more like an extended family, like, mothers and so forth. They took an interest in you." Mrs. Brown and her husband's only goal in pursuing the suit was for the district to provide transportation to and from the school, which was across town from where their family lived.

Black people in Topeka were not the only ones with concerns about the NAACP leadership's decision-making. In fact, the Kansas NAACP originally planned to bring the desegregation lawsuit on behalf of Wichita schools, but fierce opposition from both the branch's board and Black teachers afraid the move would threaten their livelihood forced them to move their cause to Topeka. No matter, once *Brown* became law, teachers in Wichita lost their jobs just the same as did teachers in Topeka. Neither teachers who attempted to teach in white schools nor those who taught Black children were safe. As I explore in this book, part of the implementation of integration involved school administrators firing almost half of the Black teachers in the South who had been employed before *Brown v. Board of Education* and, in concert with politicians, closing a similar percentage of schools educating Black children. It was an attack on Black schools, politics, and communities, which meant it was an attack on the pillars of Black life.

Even parents who did have concerns about the quality of their children's education were against *Brown v. Board*. Given the traumatic history of white violence against Black schools, it's no wonder some were content with the status quo. Between 1865 and 1880, white mobs burned almost 650 schools to the ground, and between the 1930s and 1960s, during the violently anti-Black era the historian Rayford Logan named "the nadir" of Black history, one scholar has estimated that several hundred Black schools were attacked by white supremacists *every month*. Sometimes the violence took the form of destroying educational materials or beating, bombing, and terrorizing any teachers, Black or white, who were willing to teach Black children. On one occasion in the 1870s in Paris, Texas, a group of white girls broke into a classroom and defecated atop the students' desks. As such, some parents were merely happy to have schools at all and were less concerned or disturbed by the fact that these were majority Black.

The tug-of-war between Black parents and leaders of the NAACP was in essence a battle pitting the safety found in Black institutions against the promise of power found in those that were white. Many Black parents did not trust in the promise that white teachers and administrators would accept their children. They had no faith that, just because there was a law requiring it, white educators would suddenly take an interest in training Black minds and inspiring them to dream in the same ways white children had always taken for granted.

Without Black teachers in the room, a majority were unsure that their babies could grow culturally tall and intellectually strong or feel secure despite access to increased taxpayer-supported opportunity.

Yet when a resident of Topeka wrote to the NAACP in the late 1940s to express concern that Black children might feel isolated and alienated in white schools, a lawyer for the organization said that if integration led to some Black children dropping out, that was okay, as "there were casualties in all social change." When Black teachers and principals said they were worried they might find themselves unemployed in desegregated systems, the leadership of the organization responded that this, too, was the price of change. And when some expressed worry about how total integration might negatively impact the future of Black colleges, Walter White, the NAACP's executive secretary from 1931 to 1955, said Black people needed to "give up the little kingdoms" that had developed under segregation.

What all this means is that, though the nation's oldest civil rights organizations had waged a long, complicated, and expensive war on racially segregated and unequal education, they were not representing the will of all Black people, many of whom were convinced that just adequately and equally funding the schools their children already attended was the bulk of what was needed. The writer Zora Neale Hurston, a native Floridian, prophetically wrote in 1955 that she wondered why some were excited about "a court order for somebody to associate with me who does not wish me near them." She went on to question the reasoning of the *Brown v. Board* ruling that Black children were best educated by white teachers in predominantly white schools:

If there are not adequate Negro schools in Florida, and there is some residual, some inherent and unchangeable quality in white schools, impossible to duplicate anywhere else, then I am the first to insist that Negro children of Florida be allowed to share this boon. But if there are adequate Negro schools and prepared instructors and instructions, then there is nothing different except the presence of white people.

Indeed, the only difference between white and Black schools was the value placed on the students educated there, which manifested in abundant resources and attention. The Black people who did support *Brown* did not so much believe that the presence of white teachers or students was better for their children. They merely understood that on the other side of the well-funded, well-staffed classrooms where rich and powerful white parents sent their children lay otherwise unattainable opportunity, such as access to corporate boardrooms, political power, and generational wealth. This would prove to be true for the relative few who successfully desegrated white schools. In the 1970s, along with affirmative action making classroom seats available to Black people in colleges and universities, efforts at desegregation at the K–12 level allowed some Black students equitable access to a wider variety of educational options, jobs, and economic advancement that they had long been denied. This shift was the primary engine of social mobility for Black people in the decades after the civil rights movement.

Reams of scholarly research, newspaper reports, and anecdotal evidence make clear that in the United States, Black, brown, and Indigenous children who desegregate predominantly white, high-performing schools become Supreme Court justices, vice presidents, attorneys general, CEOs, or, in the case of one Black man, even president of the United States. They are launched into a certain stratum of society by attending schools where they are provided not only with basic amenities—functional plumbing, air conditioners that blow cool air during blistering summers, and well-maintained facilities—but also an abundance of extracurricular activities, brand-new textbooks, and college preparatory courses. Laurence Tribe, a professor of constitutional law at Harvard University, says there is a "massive body of evidence" proving that underfunded schools, disproportionately attended by Black and/or Latino children, have turned generations of children into a "permanent underclass." The opposite is also true. For Black people, attending desegregated schools created a Black elite. One truth that is perhaps simple, perhaps not, is that the integration of schools in the United States made racial progress and economic opportunity possible for a relative few Black people while making it much, much, more difficult for many to achieve.

Both integration and affirmative action, which were implemented a decade apart, have faced constant opposition and consistent dismantling, most recently demonstrated by the Supreme Court's reversal of affirmative action in college admissions in June 2023. The result is that both before and after *Brown,* an overwhelming majority of Black children in the United States have attended schools segregated by race and income. Today, the engine of integration has sputtered to a near standstill.

Brown made new law, but is *a* law the same as *the* law if few follow its mandates? What would have happened, for example, if the federal government had mandated that all cars had to have seat belts, and then some car makers simply refused to install them? This is analogous to how many communities reacted to *Brown v. Board.* It became a law in name only, in search of a constituency willing to implement it. Instead of bringing true integration, *Brown v. Board of Education* was wielded as a weapon, manipulated to allow for the mass withholding of educational access.

In the first fifteen years following the ruling, Black children were not enthusiastically accepted in white schools, or often even tepidly accepted, and Black schools remained under-resourced and -funded or were shuttered altogether. Why was it so hard to make integration a reality? White community members—including parents and elected officials—refused to allow it. Instead, they chose protest, dynamite, spit, fists, and relocation. During early integration efforts, white politicians, parents, and philanthropists led coordinated and massive efforts against the idea of integrating or sharing classrooms with Black people. They bombed schools rather than allow Black children to enter, dynamited school buses that were to have taken Black children to white schools, and sometimes rioted so enthusiastically in front of the schools Black children attempted to enter that the police, National Guard, or even the military had to be called in to stop the violence. White resistance was aided by judges and elected officials who entertained countless legal challenges to integration, often siding with its detractors, and allowed white families to withdraw from school districts containing Black people and form new, all-white districts. In the process, over the decades, white attitudes against sharing educational space with Black children have, like arteries poised to still a beating heart, hardened to the point of calcification.

There are simply no other groups of children, save perhaps those who are Indigenous, who have so regularly, vehemently, and violently had their access to a quality and equitable education denied. The battle white parents waged to ensure Black children were not educated with white children, or for that matter in equally funded segregated Black schools, became a bloodstained battlefield. Five months after the ruling, in November 1955, one person told a reporter that if the threat of closed schools was not enough to deter Black families from sending their children to white schools, "a few killings would make certain. . . ." That same year, the president of the Mississippi Bar Association declared in a public speech that "the gun and torch" were available and appropriate means to ensure the continuation of segregation in public schools. And at a meeting of the American Society of Newspaper Editors held in Washington, D.C., in April 1955, Frederick Sullens, the editor of the *Daily News* in Jackson, Mississippi, told the assembled audience, "Mississippi will not obey the decision. If an effort is made to send Negroes to school with white children, there will be bloodshed. The stains of that bloodshed will be on the Supreme Court steps." Four months later, in September 1955, the month after fourteen-year-old Emmett Till's lynching, the editor of a newspaper in Yazoo City, Mississippi, wrote, "Through the furor over the Emmett Till case we hope someone gets this over to the nine ninnies who comprise the present U.S. Supreme Court. Some of the young Negro's blood is on their hands." Mike Espy, a Mississippi politician who desegregated Yazoo City High School in 1969, remembers having to carry a stick with him to fend off the physical attacks he often faced when the teacher left the room.

The first Black student to walk, diploma in hand, across a stage in a white school in the South, Bobby Cain, did so in 1957 in Clinton, Tennessee. Collectively called the Clinton 12, Cain enrolled at Clinton High School in 1956 with eleven other Black children, one of two seniors set to graduate at the end of that year. Alfred Williams, who was meant to graduate with Bobby, withdrew before the year ended after facing regular harassment and violence. On that first day in August 1956, they had all walked down the hill outside the high school together, clothes pressed and shoes shined, clutching their books and smiling as they headed into their new school. The first sign of the trouble ahead was the sound and then the sight of a threateningly large and angry crowd of white protesters chanting, yelling, and shaking signs at the children. Other residents became violent, attacking the cars of any Black people driving through the town. Tennessee governor Frank G. Clement quickly called for the assistance of the National Guard—the first but not the last time troops were required to keep Black children safe as they tried to enter a white school. It took days, but finally some semblance of order was restored, and the Black teenagers were able to enter the school building and begin attending classes. But those children, their families, and other Black community members were targets of so much sustained harassment, had so many fights, and received so many death threats that only two students were able to stick it out: Bobby and Gail Ann Epps, who graduated the year after Bobby. In October 1958, the fall after Gail received her diploma, white community members placed dynamite in the school, demolishing it. It took two years to rebuild. Once rebuilt, it would be almost a decade before any other Black children tried to attend the school. This type of violent intimidation was not an isolated incident.

On the day the Supreme Court handed down the *Brown* decision, a twelve-year-old little girl named Melba Beals was at Paul Laurence Dunbar Elementary in Little Rock, Arkansas. She wrote an autobiography decades later that included her memories of the day the *Brown* decision was announced. Fearing white rage, teachers let Melba and the other Black students out of school hours before the regular end of the school day. The early dismissal did not spare her. As she walked home, a white man, a father, chased her up a desolate street, threw her to the ground, ripped her underpants, and, before a passerby forcibly stopped him from going further, took off his belt and began pulling down his pants while yelling that he was teaching her a lesson for wanting to go to school with his white children.

Melba survived that act of sexual assault, and a few years later, she signed up to become one of the Little Rock Nine, a group of Black teenagers who were tapped to desegregate Central High School in 1957. The Little Rock cohort received far more national attention than did the travails of the Clinton 12, in part due to the open defiance of the *Brown* decision by the Arkansas governor Orval Faubus, who ordered the state's National Guard to block the students' entrance. White parents and children stood outside the school screaming and cursing, and the spectacle—quickly dubbed "The Crisis in Little Rock"—was broadcast on television for the nation to see. All howled racial epithets and threatened beatings, lynching, and sexual violation. The resistance was so staunch that President Eisenhower was forced to call out the 101st Airborne army regiment to ensure that Black students could even enter the building. Once the presence of soldiers and combat-ready weaponry guaranteed the children's entry, each was assigned a soldier to help them evade the constant attacks. Evasion was their only option because their orders precluded the soldiers from touching or in any way physically confronting any white students, teachers, staff, or administrators. Even with soldiers following them around, two members of the Little Rock Nine had dynamite thrown at them on school grounds, a white classmate hurled acid at one young woman's face, and teachers and students alike chased, harassed, and attacked them, both physically and verbally.

Economic violence and intimidation were also weapons used to make sure Black parents understood that equal education would not easily be given to their children, no matter the law. In South Carolina, once news of the decision in the *Brown v. Board* lawsuit became public, those who had been involved in the case became targets for retaliation. Reverend Joseph Armstrong DeLaine, who had rallied Black community members to sign on to the case, was fired from his job as a teacher at a local high school. School officials also fired his wife, Mattie, from her job as a school principal at a Black middle school. Their family members were also targeted. Soon after the ruling, the owners of Fleming-DeLaine funeral home, one of whom was Reverend DeLaine's nephew, learned that Black sharecroppers on some farms were no longer allowed to bring their dead to him for burial. On one occasion, a family brought in their infant for burial only to return to retrieve the child soon after, because their white employer, who had previously agreed to pay the bill, refused to pay anyone with the last name of DeLaine.

Another couple who had signed on, Harry and Eliza Briggs, both lost their jobs. Harry, who had worked as a gas station attendant for sixteen years, recalled:

> There didn't seem to be much danger to it. But after the petition was signed, I knew it was different. The white folks got kind of sour. They asked me to take my name off the petition. My boss, he said did I know what I was doin' and I said, "I'm doin' it for

the benefit of my children." He didn't say nothin' back. But then later—it was the day before Christmas—he gave me a carton of cigarettes and then he let me go. He said, "Harry, I want me a boy—and I can pay him less than you."

Briggs's wife, Eliza, cleaned rooms at the local hotel. She said her employers "told me that they were under a lot of pressure to get me and one of the other women working there to take our names off the petition." But Eliza Briggs's name was not even on the petition. When they told her that she'd better tell her husband to take his off, she responded that he had a mind of his own. They told her she no longer had a job. After they got fired, Harry and Eliza tried farming for a living. That failed once the local bank cut off their credit. Harry drove up to Sumter, a town about twenty miles away, and got a bank loan. But when the bank officers found out Harry Briggs was part of the *Brown* case, they immediately called in the loan. Later, when the family's cow broke loose, knocking over a gravestone in a local cemetery, policemen came and arrested the cow. Twenty-two other Black parents who had signed on to the lawsuit lost their jobs, too.

To be clear, it wasn't only in the South that white people, parents, and communities refused to share their schools with Black children. In April 1964, thousands of white people, mostly mothers, in New York City marched from Brooklyn to Manhattan to protest the school board's modest plans to bus Puerto Rican and Black students to predominantly white schools. In Michigan, Klan members bombed school buses sitting in a lot on the morning before they were to take Black children to schools slated for desegregation. And white parents reshaped municipal areas all over the nation by picking up and moving far away from cities with Black people so their children could attend schools with other white children. I could go on at length about the terror, beatings, threats, lost jobs, and even kidnapped pets associated with the organized and massive resistance white parents waged against

Black children attending schools with their offspring. Sharing this history does not generally make me popular at dinner parties.

My point here is that before any of the children who chose to participate in southern desegregation efforts took their first steps into white schools, parents and activists had to teach children as young as six, in the case of Ruby Bridges, who desegregated an elementary school in New Orleans, to suppress their humanity so as not to react to the violence, spit, taunts, hatred, and white rage that accompanied their attempts to desegregate white schools, much of which was captured in Pulitzer Prize–winning photographs. These violent upheavals lasted for decades, and even if Black parents in the South *wanted* to send their children back to the segregated Black schools *Brown* was supposed to have fixed, these had long been dismantled and the teachers displaced.

The dream of a taxpayer-supported public school system available to all became a tale of two systems: an underfunded public system mostly attended by Black students and another made up of public and newly opened private schools set up for and populated by white children. Congress eventually had to legislate consequences for states refusing to comply with the decision. The Civil Rights Act of 1964 enabled federal officials to withhold funding from segregated schools, which allowed the federal government to quickly respond to southern attempts to evade integration. By the end of 1966, the administration had terminated federal funds for thirty-two southern school districts that refused to end racial segregation in schools. It did not do the same for any segregated systems in any other region of the country, despite high levels of racial segregation in the North, West, and Midwest, claiming that only southern schools were required to implement *Brown.*

The effects of this resistance are felt to this day—having become a churning, roiling, untamed thing; a fast-moving river of hate, violence, and murderous rage that over the decades has risen and receded but never abated. At least one research project suggests that the way we integrated schools in the United States might have led white people impacted by integration efforts to be less, not more, likely to support public policies aimed at lessening racism in public policy. In a 2021 study tracking racial and political attitudes among nearly eleven thousand white people from 159 counties across the United States, Mark Chin, a doctoral student at Harvard who was on a fellowship at Brown University's Annenberg School of Educational Policy, found that participants who had attended schools that had abided by court-ordered desegregation mandates between the 1950s and 1980s were the most negative in their appraisals of Black children, the idea of integration, and social programs designed to aid integration overall. This group was also less likely to describe themselves as politically liberal or to send their own children to schools with high levels of non-white children. Though negative views were widespread, the most negative of Black people and of desegregation were held by participants who lived in districts where white parents most vigorously protested having Black children attend schools with their kids.

Over the past few decades, whenever asked by pollsters what they make of segregation being so ubiquitous in the United States, between 65 and 75 percent of participants across race, region, and gender say it is wrong, inequitable, and unjust. But when asked what administrators, teachers, families, and communities should do about it, the majority also seem to oppose every impactful solution. They do not want to mandate busing to try to achieve racial or economic balance. They do not approve of forcing suburbs to be part of solving metropolitan-wide problems of inequality. They do not support any solutions that *require* white parents to comply. Integration was supposed to enhance education for Black children and fix the problems associated with segregation and its ills, but seventy years after segregated schools were declared unconstitutional, we know that if integration is medicine, it is so rare, its price so high, and its taste too bitter for so many that we as a nation would rather be sick than swallow the dose.

As was true in the past, today school closings and teacher dismissals in overwhelmingly Black urban areas are still common—as is the practice of assuring Black, brown, and poor people that it is in their best interest to do without both. This is a point that was reinforced for me a few years ago when I found myself engaged in a conversation about public education with an Uber driver in New Orleans. The Orleans Parish School Board had a few weeks earlier voted to convert the last remaining public school in the city to a charter school. Founded in 1917, McDonogh 35 was the first public high school in the entire state dedicated to the education of Black children. Though some today might dismiss it as a classic Jim Crow–era relic in need of a heaping dose of educational integration, what I learned through that conversation and others was that this was a school with an outsize significance in the hearts, minds, and histories of New Orleanians of color. It was beloved by its alumni, and before Hurricane Katrina, both state and federal education officials repeatedly cited the school for academic excellence. In the aftermath of the natural disaster, one of a man-made variety followed when all the public school teachers in the city—80 percent of whom were Black—were fired. Only half of the Black teachers were ever rehired. For Black people, integration policies and practices have often meant a narrowing of high-quality choices. Or as the Columbia University scholar Sonya Horsford has put it, a "false choice," whereby court-ordered integration has meant sending Black children to white schools "that lacked access to caring and demanding teachers, institutional and interpersonal caring, and the communal bonds that existed in exclusively Black schools under segregation."

I began to think about writing this book following the publication of my 2016 book, *Cutting School: Privatization, Segregation, and the End of Public Education,* which explored the profit to be found in the chronic undereducation of non-white children in the United States. In the years following its publication, I have had many opportunities to speak at events with overwhelmingly Black and Latino audiences who wanted to talk about the system of educational apartheid their children experienced. At the time, I enthusiastically supported the idea that an integrated education was the best way to address educational inequality. When I said so, I repeatedly heard questions from parents, grandparents, and caregivers in the various audiences asking why I thought integration would fix educational inequality. For them, the trauma their children experienced in predominantly white schools and from white teachers was sometimes more harmful than the undereducation occurring in segregated schools. I have now heard this question so many times that I know it is time to think more about how and why we integrate schools in the United States. This book helps explain how it came to be that while so many accept without question that educational integration is an uncomplicated success story, they do so at the expense of others who experience it as something akin to a wrecking ball that crashed through their communities and, like a pendulum, continues to swing. Many now note that as often as it elevates some children to the highest branches on the tree of success, integration is also a strategy that leaves instability and destruction in its wake.

I began to learn this history one day when I was home from college in Florida in the late 1980s, and my grandmother started telling me pieces of a story about how early integration and desegregation realities and efforts had impacted our own family. When they met, my grandmother was a young teacher and my grandfather an ambitious educator and activist in the Jim Crow South. My grandfather believed Black educators and schools were as important to the civil rights and freedom struggle as were Black pastors and the church, because both were institutions built for Black people, by Black people. My father, an only child, had graduated from the racially segregated Pinellas High as the class president and valedictorian. He went to the historically Black Howard University, where he double-majored in philosophy and economics and was consistently on the dean's list. Upon graduation, he landed at San Francisco's Golden Gate College School of Law, and that is when everything changed. He was a member of one of the first classes to include more than one or two Black people, and it was his only experience with teachers who did not believe he could succeed. It was his first time bringing his whole self to an institution ambivalent about its responsibility to what scholar W. E. B. Du Bois termed America's "darker races." This is also when my father's drinking became both a refuge and a problem that for decades afterward he was powerless to control. While he had thrived in Black communities and schools, as part of early integration efforts at a predominantly white institution, his demons—as my grandmother described the drinking that began when he was a teenager navigating the aftermath of Emmett Till's murder—overwhelmed him. She wondered exactly what and who had failed him.

My grandparents knew that a Black child in a white world was vulnerable but thought they had prepared him to compete, strengthened him enough to withstand. They had sent their best, their beloved, over that racial wall, but instead of accepting his presence and assuming intellect and competence, the white people on the other side spit him back up like a piece of meat poorly digested. Of course, others managed the transition from segregated to desegregated. But my father couldn't. And there are others like him, those who for one reason or another could not complete the integration journey. We just don't tell their stories very often.

Though he never finished law school, from the rubble of that incompletion, my father somehow made his way back to Washington, D.C., and to an opportunity to host a new television show called *Roundabout*—an educational experiment in educating poor Black children in urban areas using television. The show was a precursor of the beloved children's program *Sesame Street,* which was also meant to prepare preschool-aged Black children for kindergarten. As efforts to integrate public schools moved from the South to the North, policymakers abandoned the idea that educational equality was an obligation the federal government owed to Black citizens. The national commitment to laws and public policies providing an equal, integrated education to Black children, which had been codified into law only a decade before my father arrived in D.C., had by then morphed into a certainty that educational access and achievement were individual problems for Black families to solve in their homes, with television as an aid.

On *Roundabout,* my father found himself serving as a role model for Black viewers, who the show's producers assumed had no male figures in their lives and came from broken, dysfunctional, uneducated, female-headed households who derided educational attainment and watched television all day. Newspaper articles written about the show said he was hired because he grew up in a similar neighborhood as the children at whom the show was aimed and therefore had an intimate understanding of what these young people needed to see to thrive. Of course, none of this was true. He had not grown up poor. Both his parents had been college educated. Both his parents remained together in his home until death separated them. But this didn't matter. By the mid-1960s, as both dreams and efforts to integrate schools faded, in their wake an idea about Black children needing saving from their families and communities took hold and became part of the landscape of educational solutions.

By the early 1970s, burgeoning social science research about the perceived violence and dysfunction in Black communities emboldened politicians and school officials to openly ask if increasing policing and programs for juvenile delinquents were not better policy options for Black children than desegregated or integrated schools. According to the Harvard historian Elizabeth Hinton, the aspersions cast on the family structures, culture, and mental abilities of Black children during that time had a dehumanizing effect. Policing metastasized as politicians, social scientists, and policymakers concluded that Black people, including children, needed less integration, more segregation, and much, much more law and order.

I know this firsthand because, for one year in the mid-1970s, I saw these national shifts play out while attending a high-poverty middle school filled with children who looked like me and where white students were in short supply. It was a building without charm or windows in what was then a poor neighborhood of San Francisco named Potrero Hill. Because of my family's custody arrangement, from the age of five I spent alternating years living between San Francisco and Clearwater, Florida. And that year in San Francisco, I found myself in a school environment in which I knew the names of more of the police officers roaming the halls than I did of the rotating cast of teachers who arrived and disappeared in increasingly short intervals.

My educational story was one of transition, neither wholly segregated nor fully integrated. When I was in the fifth grade, I desegregated a white elementary school in Florida and learned that overwhelmingly white educational settings *could* be a path for a few Black people, if we competed educationally and didn't confront or otherwise unsettle white people or seem to want to threaten the social order. There, I turned my bookishness and comfort with academic engagement into a kind of currency that would eventually "buy" me the opportunity to compete for social advancement. We who desegregate white schools learn early how not to disrupt or displease. We learn that the price for opportunity and success is the spectacular loneliness of being one of a few. These two adjacent experiences helped me understand the difference between when schools are meant to boost status and access and when they are designed to trap and impede.

My son, Jelani, attended the former type of school, with students of all races and numerous ethnicities in Princeton, New Jersey, where he grew up. There is only one public middle school and high school, so all children attending public schools in the district attended the same school during those years. The first month he was in middle school, despite scoring well on tests and in his elementary school math class, he was placed in a lower-performing educational track along with the vast majority of Black and Latino students in the building. The placement would have kept him from taking either math or science classes required by elite colleges and universities. In the time it took my husband and me to have him reassessed and moved, he developed a simmering anger about what it would cost him to be in the school's "accelerated" classes, including being separated from his closest Black friends. In his new classes, where he was the only Black child and only Black friend to his white peers, and the only one invited to sleepovers, birthday parties, or family vacations, he became an "only lonely."

Only lonelies are not the integrating Black children of the 1950s and 1960s, who had to wipe the dripping spit from their bodies as they tried to enter their school buildings. They don't require hardened military personnel to protect and guard their bodies from threats or help them withstand hurled curse words, which often land harder and strike more deeply at the softest spots of their humanity than the rocks and bottles thrown at the parts of them that would heal. Instead, they are those who were bused to wealth and whiteness and often tracked into gifted and talented, honors, or advanced-placement classes where they were either the only, or one of few, non-white children.

I have been teaching in Ivy League schools for almost thirty years, and I sometimes ask my students how many of them took advanced classes in their high schools. Almost all the hands shoot up. When I ask how many of them had Black or Latino students in their classes, maybe half will remain raised. Then I ask who had more than two Black or Latino children in any class during their four years of high school, and usually all hands glide down to their laps. Nationwide, while almost 25 percent of white students take AP exams, fewer than 10 percent of Black students do, and they are often only lonelies. Highly visible in their school photos, they are the lone faces staring out of class pictures, which I think of as desegregation portraits. I have one from the fifth grade, in which I stand in the rear, taller and darker than the other children, unsmiling. By the time he graduated high school, Jelani was one of only two Black children in the academically rigorous honors/AP college track at his school and had developed an exceptionally thick skin from years of having to repeatedly steady himself in public after hearing "the N word" drip from the lips of his friends and classmates with ease, set to music, in jest, and sometimes in anger.

My son told me once when he was in high school that he had to learn to "put on a face" to protect parts of himself from prying eyes, another way of saying he learned how to "wear the mask," an allusion to a poem by Paul Laurence Dunbar that begins:

We wear the mask that grins and lies,
It hides our cheeks and shades our eyes,— ...
With torn and bleeding hearts we smile ...

His scars have healed. We both survived, and desegregation made class mobility and societal opportunity much more possible for us both. But integration is a policy cure that, like some cancer treatments, is a cure of a killing kind. My telling of the story of the rise and then fall of support for educational desegregation and integration policies and the assault on equity this turnabout represents is focused through a lens that is personal and familial, contemporary and historical. I believe it is worth telling because the road toward the nation fully realizing its professed ideals of inclusive democracy and robust citizenship requires Black people to have access to well-funded classrooms and high-quality, nurturing teachers.

McDonogh, the beloved institution that was converted to a charter school in New Orleans, was segregated both before and after the hurricane hit. But the version left behind was not one that fostered Black community or nurtured and healed the hurts inflicted by a majority-white society. And while the schools many of the displaced Black children attended were also overwhelmingly Black, the teachers were not, and the educational outcomes bore no relationship to those at schools like McDonogh. Most tragic is that many Black children who attended McDonogh and other schools in New Orleans after the mass firing never knew that there had been a time when their schools had once been full of children who were taught that they were enough as they were. Or where their shared games and laughter, dreams and hurts, tears and language marked them as more than fellow humans, but as kin. Too few today know education was ever a form of Black love, could be the practice of Black joy—that Black children could learn on the threshold of welcome. Instead, over time, Black children were taught that if they were to learn and rise, it would be despite their Black skin, families, and communities.

In our present moment, districts in major metropolitan areas like Chicago, New York, Philadelphia, Miami, Los Angeles, and Dallas have schools that are overwhelmingly segregated by race and economic levels. The majority of Black and Latino schools in cities remain underfunded, the children in them struggle educationally, and segregation today is worse in the West and Midwest than in the South. Segregation takes many forms, wears many faces, exists in both the South and the North, and has always impacted middle- and upper-class Black people as well as those who are poor or working class. Class does not in fact function as some sort of kryptonite for anti-Blackness when it is wrapped up in educational violence. It's not easier to navigate the unequal, race-impacting policies and strategies affecting schools when one is middle or upper middle class. It's just different. What this means is that, even in integrated schools, middle-class Black children and their parents quickly come to learn there is a glue felt but not quite clearly seen sticking Black children in lower-performing classrooms.

When we ask them, students say segregated, tracked, unequal, and underfunded schools, and the education received in them, constitute an underacknowledged form of structural racism that, over time, harms them as surely as do physical forms of violence. Children and adolescents tell us stories of feeling alienated and unwelcomed in the majority-white schools they attend. We point out and decry these events but do little to explain how, even within schools that have somewhat equal numbers of children from different racial and ethnic backgrounds, poor children, Black children, and Latino children are disciplined, suspended, medicated, and tracked into an undesirable caste of second-class citizenship and anemic opportunities. We know these things happen, but there is a more complete story in need of telling, a recounting requiring us to open historical and contemporary ledger books that we rarely acknowledge exist.

I don't know when the day will dawn, but I believe a morning will come when we as a nation collectively toast our wrestled defeat of inequitable education, which has for generations benefited or punished based on skin color and determined access to high-paying jobs, college degrees, and home equity. On that day, I hope we struggle to remember why the powerful and wealthy in the United States created, allowed, and then largely ignored an educational system so starkly divided and debilitating that a child, like the young girl who sat in a classroom with a paper clip, would conclude that she needed to shed one skin, grow another, and start her educational life anew to advance.

Before that future can find us, we who believe that educational equality is a requirement for a healthy democracy will need to fully acknowledge the failure of the dream of shared access to resources and intuitional governance that was to have been complete integration. We will have to speak the reality of how educational segregation continues to cement caste at the high and low ends of the status spectrum in the United States. We will need to teach the truth of how desegregation has benefited small percentages of Black, Latino, Indigenous, and poor children in such spectacular ways that we celebrate their becoming elected officials, award-winning journalists for top media outlets, captains of industry, and scholars with endowed chairs at elite universities. We will have to say we were so dazzled by the heights they scaled, we rarely noted how the visible success of the desegregators required forgetting or choosing not to see the quicksand sucking children who are unluckily segregated down and out of view. I have begun to wonder if we should require "impact statements" such as those found in some environmental policies to go along with the educational policies we propose when we say we want to specifically help poor students who are Black and Latino survive. Perhaps thinking about education as health of the civic, economic, and political kind could set our feet on a path leading toward holistically nurtured children and schools and away from classrooms where segregation and underfunding lead young hands and tender hearts to believe if they removed their skin they would have better schools.

I include my family's story to illustrate both the geographic and familial impact of segregated, desegregated, and integrated education on Black people in the United States. Integrated educational spaces harm, and segregation continues to hurt. My goal is to show the personal and national consequences of an educational justice arc that bent from segregated to desegregated and then back again and to explore the psychic price of experiencing, surviving, or failing to survive integration on communities, politics, and children. The sum of the debt owed may remain forever unknown, but I know the price is high. My family and I are at ease in predominantly white settings. We are not segregated. That is not the whole of the story. The rest is told in this book.

1

"IT IS THROUGH OUR CHILDREN WE WILL BE FREE."

In March 2021, less than a year after the American Medical Association acknowledged racism as a public health threat, a law firm specializing in civil rights filed the country's first lawsuit claiming students had a right to an anti-racist education. Filed on behalf of Integrate-NYC, a youth-led organization that fights for equity in schools, the harms listed in the lawsuit were educational, psychological, emotional, spiritual, and physical: decrepit and unfit buildings compared to those in wealthier, less brown and Black schools; uncaring teachers; and curriculums that excluded positive mentions of people who looked like them. The lawsuit recounts how often Black and Latino students encountered vermin such as rats and cockroaches in classrooms and hallways. One New York City student said they had been tasked by their teacher with killing a rat that made its way into the class. Students at a majority-Black and low-income school placed adjacent to a busy freeway described feeling regularly unfocused and numb and struggling to concentrate or speak in class over the constant din of traffic.

Over the years, the teenage plaintiffs said, recognition dawned that they were part of a school system that treated them, and those with Black and brown skin generally, differently than it treated those who were white or Asian—they surmised because Black and brown people were somehow less worthy of cleanliness, safety, and care. "Children of color, in particular, experience and internalize the racism that is inherent in their educational experiences, which in turn hinders their educational achievement," the lawsuit read. The type of racism the lawsuit described was not about an individual who held discriminatory thoughts and intent and inflicted both on students. It was not about a teacher who blocked a student's access to a special program or a principal who meted out discipline haphazardly. It was about an entire system designed to deliver subpar educational experiences to children who are Black and Latino. These students were talking about how racism and discrimination are embedded in the functioning of institutions and structures. They were describing structural racism, the "downstream consequences" of which strongly impact individual health, according to the author and psychiatrist Jonathan Metzel.

The term structural racism was coined in 1968 by Stokely Carmichael, the civil rights era activist who would later change his name to Kwame Ture. Speaking to a group of mental health practitioners and social workers at an annual professional meeting for social workers held in New York City, Ture urged them to stop focusing on racism in terms of individual actions or beliefs and instead see it as embedded in the way social structures and institutions functioned, as part of these systems' DNA. "I don't deal with the individual. I think it's a copout when people talk about the individual," he said. Instead, he pushed the group to devise a treatment plan for the silent, malignant racism of "established and respected forces in the society" that worked to maintain the status quo through structures such as zoning laws, economic policies, welfare bureaucracies, school systems, criminal law enforcement, and courts. Structural and institutionalized racism, he argued, "is less overt, far more subtle, less identifiable in terms of specific individuals committing the acts but is no less destructive of human life."

Though ultimately dismissed, which prevented the issues it raised from being robustly debated in public, the IntegrateNYC lawsuit shed light on the widespread and harmful effects of systemic racism on the city's segregated school system and its students. "If the government's goal were to create a system of education that would replicate and in fact exacerbate pernicious racial inequality in the City, it would be challenging to design a more effective system than that which currently exists," the lawsuit read. According to 2019 school diversity research on the New York City Council website, between 2010 and 2019, close to 75 percent of Black and Latino students in New York City attended schools with less than 10 percent white students, while nearly 35 percent of white students attended schools with majority-white populations. It's the most segregated school system for Black students and the second most for Latino students—conditions that, the anti-racism lawsuit lawyers argued, placed the comfort of white parents and politicians over the needs of non-white children. It took more than fifty years, but public discourse had finally caught up to Ture.

Racism is a toxic force that harms most everything in its path, especially children sitting in school buildings. In fall 2020, the American Medical Association, as well as various schools, organizations, and local municipal agencies dedicated to public health, all proclaimed the racism inherent in educational, economic, and social disparities a health threat. In expressing support of the AMA, a researcher for the NAACP Legal Defense Fund put it more forcefully: "Structural racism is a public health crisis." Given the stories of vermin-infested classrooms, noise pollution, and unsound buildings in the lawsuit, it's not a stretch to position segregated and underfunded schools as a health hazard, or structural racism as the culprit. The potential impacts of these conditions are well-documented. According to a 2020 World Health Organization report, for instance, long-term exposure to noise such as that endured by the students learning next to a busy freeway can contribute to a variety of health effects, including sleep disturbance, negative effects on the cardiovascular and metabolic system, and "cognitive and reading impairment" in children. And the U.S. Environmental Protection Agency has reported that proximity to vermin can lead to chronic absenteeism and asthma in students.

But perhaps the most pernicious and urgent impact of the systemic racism of the educational ecosystem is the mental turmoil and distress it causes in Black children. Children attending racially and economically segregated public schools say the curriculum, teachers, buildings, and expectations in their schools teach them that they have limited worth. Though they were told to study hard as a way out of the impacts of educational segregation, reading the lawsuits filed by students in New York City makes clear that differences in educational infrastructure, resources, quality, and outcomes, as well as recognition of the lack of music, art, and sports programs or quality materials, were shaping the self-concepts of too many children, leading them to believe that, as one student plaintiff put it, "you don't matter." This is a refrain as easily muttered by students in schools in Trenton and similarly under-performing systems like Detroit, as well as by Black students in integrated and high-performing districts like Princeton. The impact, the lawyers alleged, is that children who were not white internalized the racism that is inherent in their educational experiences and did not feel that they were equal. They wondered about a system that would treat them one way, and white and Asian students another way entirely. That is what structured racial inequality looks like. That is how it works. And it is hard to overcome. That is why the lawsuit demanded not only improved conditions and treatment in the schools but also, and most important, an educational experience that was actually and actively anti-racist.

Of course, lawyers, teachers, and scholars have long known that there are negative health impacts associated with segregated, unequal, and underfunded schools. Indeed, in its *Brown v. Board of Education* decision, the Supreme Court cited research published by psychologists Mamie and Kenneth Clark in a 1950 paper concluding that "to separate [African American children] from others of similar age and qualifications solely because of their race generates a feeling of inferiority as to their status in the community that may affect their hearts and minds in a way unlikely ever to be undone." Drs. Clark used four dolls, identical in every way except complexion, to test children's racial perceptions. Their subjects, children between the ages of three and seven, were asked to identify both the race of the dolls and which color doll they preferred. Most of the children, including those who were Black, preferred the white doll and assigned it positive characteristics. The Clarks concluded that "prejudice, discrimination, and segregation" created a feeling of inferiority in Black children. In other words, racism had a negative impact on their mental health.

In 2019, a year before lawyers in New York filed their suit, students in Detroit expressed a similar sense of inferiority in a suit lambasting the state for the dismal conditions in the city's schools and its failure to properly educate its students, with one sixteen-year-old student plaintiff saying her school environment "made me feel less than zero." Ninety-nine percent of children in Detroit are Black and Latino, and 93 percent of them attended schools with buildings so decrepit that during the 2016–2017 school year, *none* met health and safety codes. One of the ways the student plaintiffs argued their case about having been failed by their school system was by showing that building temperatures in many schools regularly hovered at ninety degrees, no matter the season or temperature outside. On the first day of school in 2016, filings in the case showed, the heat was so bad that several teachers and students in multiple schools threw up, while others passed out. At the other end of the spectrum, when the schools were not overheated, these were so cold that, in the winter, teachers and students could see their breath hanging in the air when they exhaled. They wore coats, hats, scarves, gloves, and layers of clothes to withstand the low temperatures. In addition to the issues with the heating and cooling systems, the plaintiffs in the Detroit case provided evidence that mice, roaches, and "other vermin" regularly inhabited their classrooms. Teachers reported having grown accustomed to cleaning up rodent feces in the morning before their students arrived. In a few schools, the plaintiffs alleged, the infrastructure was in such disrepair and plumbing leaks so frequent that they spent class time keeping an eye on the ceilings to avoid falling tiles. Even the water in many buildings was found to have been so contaminated with pollutants that it was unsafe to drink. "I don't feel anymore," said one sixteen-year-old-plaintiff. "It's painful and infuriating. It tears you down piece by piece every single day."

In some Detroit schools, class sizes swelled to fifty or sixty students in classrooms that contained enough desks for only forty, the supposed maximum. When that happened, students sat on the floor or stood along the walls when class was in session. Teacher shortages meant that on some days, students could spend up to three class periods per day in the gym. As a means of drawing attention to the lack of adequate staffing in her school, one teacher had taken to standing in front of the building handing out flyers urging parents to "ask your child if they had a teacher today." In perhaps the most notable example of the severity of the teaching shortages in the district, at one school, "eighth-grade students were put in charge of teaching seventh and eighth grade math classes for a month because no math teacher was available." A student in one of these schools said, "It's hard being a Black girl. They expect us to take this and not show any emotion. And if we do, WE are called crazy and WE are treated like we are crazy." Talking to a documentary filmmaker about the case, one of the plaintiffs summed things up, saying, "You are left in the hands of people who have never been to your neighborhood, to your school, probably never having been to your city and they get to choose our education."

Despite the many disturbing revelations included in the suit, at its core was a rudimentary demand: that students be taught basic reading comprehension. In 2019, the year the lawsuit was filed, less than a quarter of fourth-grade and 39 percent of eighth-grade students in

Detroit public schools met even the basic standards of literacy as measured by the National Assessment of Educational Progress, while only 7 and 6 percent, respectively, tested as proficient—significantly less than any other major city. Literacy levels have been a long-standing problem in the city, with students consistently ranking lower than the national standard and proficiency rates hovering at or under 7 percent since 2009. "How can you expect someone, anyone in our country to be engaged in civics or the process at all if they can't even read?" Helen Moore, the community activist who, along with students, caregivers, teachers, and administrators, first approached the law firm to file the literacy suit, told a reporter. "You can't take part in our democracy unless you can read, so why is it that you have all these people working so hard to make sure Black students aren't able to read?" Moore likened the neglect to the deliberate lack of educational access for enslaved Black children centuries earlier.

The students argued that denying them access to basic literacy was an assault on their ability to act as full citizens, and that the city's schools had become a tool to separate them from the lifeblood of democracy. "We hear this all the time, 'We are the future,'" one of the student plaintiffs said. "How are we going to be the future if we don't know anything? This makes us feel discouraged. This makes us feel like we don't want to be in our communities." Though the case was ultimately settled for a relatively modest sum and without providing a much-desired legal precedent, in April 2020, a federal appeals court affirmed the students' argument that they had been "deprived of access to literacy." The court concluded that the state of Michigan was infringing on their constitutional right to an "adequate" education by denying them a skill necessary to function as citizens.

The children know something is wrong. They have been trying to tell us. They know they struggle to dream an American dream. They think the fault is theirs. I think adults are to blame. How can a school district, as one teacher in the district put it, "fail the children in their schools so spectacularly, and no one see it as a crisis?" Yet it's not so much that no one saw what was happening, it's that those who had the power to make changes simply chose not to do so. "No one ever asked us if what they have done is right, or if it is working for our children," said one parent-activist. "It's not. But no one even asked." In responding to the lawsuit, the superintendent of the public schools in Detroit at the time, who was not named in it, echoed this criticism:

> This lawsuit . . . speaks to years of educational injustice in Detroit linked to imposed governance structures that stripped the city of local control. No district in this country experienced the brutal history of what DPS endured, more importantly, what children endured. The state took over the district, without the people's consent, and the district went backwards. Adults need to be held accountable for that, and more importantly, today's children cannot suffer the same consequences.

Black people in Detroit had been ringing the alarm bells for decades—none more vigorously than Helen Moore. In 2023, Moore was eighty-seven and had lived in Detroit for eighty-four of those years. She became an educational organizer and activist in the city in 1969, when the first of her children began to attend school. By then, the factories had begun moving to the suburbs, taking many of the middle-class and white residents and their tax dollars with them. This shift initiated a downward economic slide of educational funding and quality. In 1994, noting the social, emotional, physical, financial, and psychological impact of education policies on the health of Detroit residents, community members organized a campaign to raise $1.5 billion in bond money to invest in city schools by taxing them. The funds, which would come from taxes on residents, would be used to repair dilapidated schools, build new ones, and fund needed curricular and pedagogical initiatives. Community members saw this as an opportunity to provide their children with educational facilities and curricular enhancements like those found in the suburbs and throughout the state.

Organized in defiance of the mayor of Detroit, the governor, the legislature, and the president of the teachers' union, Proposal S relied on a determined grassroots campaign. "We went door to door. We telephone banked. We went school to school, church to church—everything," Delores Smith, the head of the group, said about the work done by her and seventy-five members of the Citizens for Bond Committee. Campaign organizers encouraged voters to go to any city school and see conditions for themselves. In explaining his opposition to the bond, the president of the Greater Detroit Chamber of Commerce cited concerns "regarding the planning, management, and cost impact of a $1.5 billion program in the fragile economic situation which exists in Detroit." And John Elliott, then the president of the Detroit Federation of Teachers, questioned whether the money would be spent wisely, to which Moore responded that Mr. Elliott was "spending too much time talking to the mayor" rather than parents and students. Though politicians doubting voters' ability to identify their children's needs believed "the little people don't count," she told community members, "we are going to have to show them the power of the people."

At the time, the city had a supportive school board that had worked collaboratively with school leaders to design an innovative curriculum that included foreign languages, vocational arts, fine art, music, and college prep. At that point, according to journalists, education scholars, teachers, and community activists, Detroit schools were poised to become a model for how to transform struggling urban, majority-of-color school districts into world-class educational institutions. All they needed, organizers and school leaders said, was for voters whose kids actually attended these schools to provide the funding to solidify their vision.

Though it caught seasoned political insiders completely by surprise, the bond issue passed with 60 percent of eligible voters—the largest bond issue ever passed in the city. That it passed at all stunned state and local leaders who had refused to support it. A few years after the bond issue passed and construction and repair had begun in the schools, the folks in Detroit got even better news. In addition to a $93 million surplus in their general operating budget in 1997, their test scores had begun to rise, posting sharp gains in science and writing. Overall proficiency levels soared as well. Even the school superintendent, who had been against the bond proposal, sang a line from the James Brown song "I Feel Good" when asked about this reversal of fortune.

But by 1999, all that changed. Members of the business community, including those in construction who felt shut out of access to the $1.5 billion in bond money, took their grievances to Governor John Engler's office. They were, after all, among his largest donors. According to media coverage of the event, Engler surprised many when in a speech to the Economic Club of Detroit that year, he declared the district bankrupt, heading in the wrong direction, dilapidated, and failing and announced that he was stepping in to help. He said the changes he was about to make were not about "race, money or power" but that "the reforms were about children." His first order of action was dissolving the democratically elected school board and installing a "reform board" to save the district. This new board would, he said, report directly to him and not be responsible to the voters in the city of Detroit.

The first thing the new reform board did was determine that none of the $1.5 billion in bond money would go toward individual schools for principals to make curricular and pedagogical enhancements. No, all of it would go to construction and infrastructure. And one of the white construction firms that had taken its case to the governor was now to have sole discretion and oversight for how this money would be spent. The reform board also fired all three of the Black firms that had been slated to receive 50 percent of construction funds.

The second item on the new reform board's agenda was to pass rules limiting the amount of community input they would allow at meetings. They banned signs and protests, actions that activists and residents said were driven solely by the interests of corporations rather than the students. Over the next three years, the reform board spent all the bond money and turned a $93 million surplus into a $250 million debt.

Reflecting on the reversal, one parent-activist said, "We fight, we win, but then they take it from us, and we have to fight again. It takes a hell of a toll." Moore added, "Every time we thought things would get better, they didn't. It's like we didn't have any power." It took until 2006, but Moore and the other school and community activists organized a recall election to return school governance to an elected school board. Voters said resoundingly that they wanted to go back to an elected board to decide curriculums, policies, and budgets. But though they won the vote, within three years the $300 million debt hamstringing the district led the state, this time led by a Democratic governor, Jennifer Granholm, to again take control. Granholm appointed an emergency financial manager to address decisions about the overwhelming debt.

The first emergency financial manager, Robert Bobb, immediately claimed that his job had to extend beyond financial matters to include curriculum and personnel. The school board disagreed and filed a suit saying he had exceeded his power and authority by trying to influence academics. But just sixty days after a court victory, Rick Snyder won the race for governor, and the GOP took control of the legislature. It didn't take long for his administration to pass an Emergency Manager Law, which suspended democracy relative to school governance and gave Bobb complete control of every aspect of the school district. It stripped the school board of all its power, exempted Bobb from the Open Meetings Act, and made clear Bobb could be removed from his position only by the governor. Of course, Moore and other activists moved quickly to organize a repeal of the Emergency Manager Law, which gave governor-appointed emergency managers almost unlimited power, by referendum. Though they needed only 150,000 signatures, they submitted 204,000 signatures for certification, believing they needed to have a healthy cushion to succeed. In the end, it wasn't the number of names that was called into question, but rather the font size in the paperwork. The law required fourteen-point font rather than the 13.75 point they used, so lawmakers in Lansing threw it out.

Undeterred, the activists expanded their efforts and organized a state-wide referendum. To succeed, a majority of the eighty-one counties in Michigan needed to vote for the repeal. Everyone told the activists that there was no way they would get all those white counties to support them. In the end, seventy-seven of eighty-one counties stood with the people of Detroit and voted down the Emergency Manager Law. Two weeks later, Governor Snyder rolled out a new version of the law to replace the one that voters had rejected. He had his staff write an almost identical bill, this time adding the provision that it could not be repealed by referendum, and that each emergency manager could serve for only eighteen months each, as opposed to indefinitely. When members of the media asked about this move and its seeming intent to thwart the clear will of voters, he simply said, "We followed the law. There is no issue." To save you the ins and outs of the dizzying series of events between 2009 and 2016, there were five emergency managers overall, and the upshot of this state oversight and its various policies is that, while in 1999 Detroit had been in the middle of the educational pack relative to the United States, by 2019, it was ranked fiftieth. "This has nothing to do with our finances, and everything to do with trying to steal our democracy," said one parent-activist.

By the time the citizens of Detroit finally got back control of the schools, there was more debt than any of them could believe. Also, two hundred of the city's schools had been closed and overreliance on standardized tests had labeled whole swaths of the community as deficient, triggering various provisions of federal policy that required traditional public schools to be replaced with charter schools. This shrunk the district and drained the enrollments that would have helped Detroit remain solvent. In 2021, the district's deficit was almost $500 million and its long-term debt $1.5 billion—a sum that will take until 2038 to pay back.

Those most hurt by these policy games and cures are the children. "I know it was politics, but I felt like I wasn't smart enough, I wasn't good enough, I caused my school to close. I know it's not true, but I thought that," said one of the plaintiffs of the literacy suit. Another adds: "I want people to know that, when they come for your schools, they are coming for you." It is time to ask what social policy would look like if it were crafted with a view toward ensuring the social, mental, emotional, and physical health of those most deeply impacted by it. The sustained efforts toward dismantling education and interrupting democracy in Detroit made many of the parents and aunts and grand-parents and students in that city doubt and question not just themselves, but also elected officials, the ability of the vulnerable to ever triumph over the powerful, and, in the end, the efficacy of democracy itself. If there is triumph here, it is in the fact that there were, if even for fleeting moments, battles that were won, which is in large part due to the indefatigable spirit of Moore and others like her who fought hard for educational equity in the city. In 2020, Moore shifted her focus from education advocacy to the Electoral College, an entity she said she doesn't really understand and just learned about when she served as an elector for Michigan in that year's presidential election. Reflect-ing on the experience, she said, "Maybe I'm missing something, but why can't we just allow the voters' decision to stand? All this extra stuff seems to make the process more complicated than it needs to be."

This joining of voting rights and educational rights is interest-ing to me because there are similar, if less extreme, stories of educa-tional neglect in highly segregated, postindustrial cities in the South,

Midwest, and East Coast with large populations of Black and Latino students in their school systems. Interestingly, all the cities whose vote counts we waited breathlessly for in order to determine the winner of the 2016 presidential election—Atlanta, Detroit, Milwaukee—have stories about the health impacts of the past three decades of educational policies promising that there would be "No Child Left Behind"; that they could compete to "Race to the Top"; and that "Every Student Succeeds." Each has left teachers and community members and activists in a steady state of protest and pushback. If we asked people like Helen Moore to write our legislative future, I am sure it would look very different. As Moore says, "It is through our children we will be free." But first, I would add, we need to keep our children healthy and safe.

Today, we all should know the costs of racial and economic segregation in education are physical, emotional, financial, and social. The situation is dire. In 2021, the Economic Policy Institute found that "unaddressed school segregation" remains a major and long-standing policy failure that continues to consign most Black children to schools that put them behind academically. We know about the high and persistent hurdles segregation imposes on non-white children and about the damage underfunded segregated schools have caused from well before *Brown v. Board of Education* to today. Fewer Black families can afford to live in neighborhoods with high property values and well-financed neighborhood schools, so Black and Latino kids disproportionately experience the brunt of the "downstream consequences" of racism, both inside and outside schools. I could go on, but I want to give Moore the last word here: "Listen, there wouldn't be a Black person in the United States if all of us had stopped and said, 'Oh, we can't do this anymore. Just kill us and fall dead.' So, we're still here, and as long as we're still here, we got a chance of being free."

THE ROAD TO SEGREGATION

An uncomfortable yet enduring truth is that far too few Black children have had consistent access to the version of public education the nation's founders envisioned. Thomas Jefferson, John Adams, and other early leaders first proposed the creation of a formal system of publicly funded schools after the American Revolution, believing basic education to be the only chance of survival for their new experiment in self-governing models of democracy. In 1787, as the boundaries of the new nation pushed westward, the nation's congress enacted the Northwest Ordinance to prohibit slavery spreading west and provide parameters for new states and territories entering the United States. "Religion, morality, and knowledge, being necessary to good government and the happiness of mankind, schools and the means of education shall forever be encouraged," the ordinance read, establishing the basic framework for a public education system. While some Northeastern communities did establish publicly funded or free schools, the concept did not begin to take hold on a wider scale until the 1830s. That is when Horace Mann, a Massachusetts legislator and secretary of that state's board of education, once again proposed the creation of a state-funded public school system that would be available to all children free of charge and teach the basics of reading, math, and civics. Mann and other proponents of "common schools," as he termed them, viewed these schools as an investment that would eventually benefit the whole nation—the first step to helping the future electorate learn the responsibilities of citizenship. The common school dream was for all children across race and status, middle class, poor, immigrant, or native born, to meet each other in schools and learn to respect each other, facilitating a shared cultural identity as Americans. Racial segregation was not part of the vision, yet from the beginning, it compromised common school proponents' inclusive ideals.

Indeed, the exclusion of non-white students from public schools spans the nation, stretches across time periods, and is broad, deep, and wide. The first-ever lawsuit decrying race-based exclusion from a publicly funded school in the United States was filed by a Black parent in Boston, the home of the common school movement, in 1848. But it wasn't just Black students who were excluded from public schools. In some states and communities, Latino and Chinese American students were also forbidden from sitting in classrooms with white children. Indigenous children, not generally accepted into common schools either, were sent to federally run day or boarding schools, where the goal was to assimilate them into white culture and discourage them from embracing their own histories, families, and language. The intent for Black and Indigenous students never seemed to be preparing them for citizenship, but rather to separate them from their families and civilize them, teaching them that they should strive to learn and succeed among people who did not think them fully human. The knotted reality of integration, segregation, and opportunity dates to the first years of the formal founding of the American republic, which our white male leaders ensured would be bound up with who should or could have what type or quality of education. At the start of this story, the main characters are Indigenous and white, and trauma and psychological abuse run rampant, as does unchecked greed.

In 1776, a man named Koquethagechton was selected by the Lenape people (members of the Delaware nation, in what we would today refer to as Ohio) to lead and represent them before the recently formed Continental Congress. At the gathering, Koquethagechton called for peace between Indigenous people and white settlers and agreed that, were the United States to go to war with the British, the Lenape would either remain neutral or aid the United States. He also proposed that Congress, instead of waging war and relying on dispossessing them of their land to fund U.S. expansion, allow Indigenous people to form a fourteenth state that would have entered the new union with full citizenship rights and property protections. Though the other members never agreed to the formation of a fourteenth state that would become an Indigenous homeland, in 1778 the Continental Congress commissioned Koquethagechton as a lieutenant colonel in its army. Within a few years, while serving as a guide for members of the army, Koquethagechton was murdered. Some suspected an unknown assailant, others Continental soldiers. But either way, with the Lenape leader dead, Congress ordered his people to arrange for Koquethagechton's son George Morgan White Eyes to be educated in the English language and to learn the ways, religion, and culture of white people in preparation for inheriting his father's position. To enact this plan, the young man was named a ward of the United States Congress, which agreed to be responsible for his educational and living expenses in acknowledgment of his father's service. Rather than send him to Dartmouth College, a school founded specifically to educate Indigenous people, the Continental Congress determined that he should attend the College of New Jersey, now known as Princeton University—the sort of white, elite environment where congressmen might send their own children.

White Eyes entered the College of New Jersey as a freshman in the fall of 1785 at fifteen years old. It is worth noting that though Congress agreed to pay for his education, unbeknownst to either White Eyes or his people, the legislative body stipulated that the Delaware people would pay for this kindness by deeding the United States ownership of a portion of their land for each year the young man attended the school. No members of the Delaware nation ever agreed to this "bargain." A couple of years later, Congress abandoned White Eyes.

On December 23, 1787, he and several other students were called before the faculty on an accusation of being rude to a tutor. Though school administrators were willing to keep the white youngsters similarly accused, they wanted White Eyes expelled. One of his supporters urged compassion, saying White Eyes might have been acting out because he'd just received news that his mother had been murdered by white men disguised as natives who robbed her of the animal skins she was bringing to sell at a market. His supporter argued that this zero-tolerance policy regarding discipline was unfair and represented a double standard, given that "his mistakes and misconduct have been far surpassed by white boys of his age, who have the superior advantage of enlightened and tender parents to guard over them." But in the end, the letter didn't matter, and the school expelled White Eyes. Devastated by this turn of events, White Eyes wrote to George Washington for help, reminding him that he was a ward of Congress and that they had pledged to support him. He pleaded:

> I am reduced at last to the disagreeable Necessity of applying for relief to your Excellency, my Situation at present being painful to the greatest Degree, better had Congress a Body for whom I have the highest Veneration left me to wander in the Wilds of my native Country than I to experience the heart breaking Sensations I now feel—Without Friends, without one I dare unbosom myself to,

am I left, & in this Situation throw myself at the Feet of your well known Goodness & beg leave to relate all the Circumstances that lead to my present Situation.

White Eyes felt he'd been disciplined more harshly than the white privileged children with whom he went to school. "I was not without faults I acknowledge," he wrote in a second letter, after not receiving a reply to the first. "But they were in my boyish days, & they are not greater than what I see committed by Children of many Parents—In me they could not be overlooked—Many a time I reflect on the happy Situation of Children who have Parents tenderly to advise them—I was deprived of that Blessing." Aside from being deprived of an education, White Eyes shared that he was penniless and found himself without food, a place to live, or enough clothing to keep warm in the winter. If he was to receive no further support, he pleaded with Washington to at least provide a job in service to the government. A job, he wrote, would give him the means to support himself.

As Congress remained mute, White Eyes again wrote to Washington saying he just wanted to go home, adding, "I believe they are tired of doing anything for me & I am tired of waiting for them to do their duty. . . ." This time, in response, Washington seems to have arranged for White Eyes to have a line of credit. At first, Alexander Hamilton at the Board of the Treasury disputed charges for his clothing, lodging, and food, which White Eyes said led him to feel "not of as much Consequence as a Dog." Finally, though it took them over a year from when the first request was made to do so, Congress authorized payment for the debts White Eyes had incurred. He returned to his people disillusioned, and a year after that he was shot to death by a white man just like his mother and father before him. In response to learning of the murder, John Witherspoon, the former chaplain of the Congress and president of the College of New Jersey/Princeton, declared an end to what he considered to have been a failed experiment in integrating Indigenous students into schools attended by the white elite. Witherspoon wrote:

> The chief thing that a philosopher can learn from the Indians in New Jersey is, that, on the whole, it does not appear, that either by our people going among them, or by their being brought among us, that it is possible to give them a relish of civilized life. There have been some of them educated at this college, as well as in New England; but seldom or never did they prove either good or useful.

Going forward, the government's strategy toward Indigenous education and assimilation took a hard turn from integration to segregation. Abandoning the idea of grooming Indigenous people for leadership positions by offering them the classical education experienced by the white elite, Congress enacted the Civilization Fund Act of 1819, which empowered the federal government to remove children from their parents and communities by force, if necessary, to educate them in a network of segregated and poorly funded boarding schools. The education on offer in those schools was designed to infuse Indigenous children with "good moral character" through vocational arts instruction, meant to teach them the value of labor as a step on the road toward being civilized. What these "Indigenous only" institutions were not at all designed to do was to affirm any aspect of their culture, encourage them to see themselves as equal to white people, or provide economic opportunity.

Between 1869 and the late 1960s, over one hundred thousand Indigenous children were taken from their families and homelands, some forcibly kidnapped by federal troops, and placed in boarding schools, where they were stripped of all things associated with their communities and cultures. Teachers at the schools cut the incoming students' long hair, a source of pride, into identical bowl haircuts. Children were forced to wear uniforms, and their days were organized by military-style regimentation. Beatings with open hands and closed fists were not uncommon, and whippings with belts and sticks were an accepted form of discipline for infractions such as speaking in one of their native tongues. Violence was so frequent and food and medical attention often so scarce that many students died from sickness or abuse. Students were forbidden from seeing or interacting with their families during the school year, so parents sometimes learned their children had died only after they had been buried in school cemeteries, some in unmarked graves.

In addition to the bleak and harsh lives they lived, the children, without their parents' consent, were leased out to white homes to perform menial labor during the summers, when they should have been allowed to go home and visit their families. School administrators justified their actions by saying the primary function of education for Indigenous children was to prepare them to be laborers. That is why Indigenous children also performed most of the work required to keep the schools functioning. They were never compensated for their work. It wasn't until the late 1970s that Congress outlawed the forced removal of Indigenous children from their families. What happened to Indigenous children proved to be a precursor of the thinking that led to Black children being bused to schools outside their communities following the *Brown v. Board* decision. The teachers and schools in Black communities were deemed unacceptable, and being separated from them was perceived as the only way for them to receive a quality education.

An early example of the approach to and mentality about the education of Black children is a school founded following the Civil War. Samuel Chapman Armstrong was a Union Army general who had been charged with leading Black men into battle as the leader of an all-Black "Colored Troop." Armstrong said that the experience inspired him to join the Freedmen's Bureau, a federal agency formed in the aftermath of the divisive conflict to deal with issues related to the formerly enslaved. And when he noticed the low literacy levels among the newly freed people, he began to take an interest in Black children's education.

Influenced by the model and example of the education of Indigenous children, Armstrong founded a vocational school to similarly educate Indigenous and Black children. The vision of education for these children was a tightly woven net with threads spun from segregation, labor, civilization, and vocational education. Armstrong insisted his students work hard but avoid politics, including steering clear of discussions about Black people being allowed to vote, even though the Fifteenth Amendment to the Constitution had given them that right. As far as he was concerned, neither group was fit to participate in political governance. He believed Indigenous people were given to savagery and that the experiences of the formerly enslaved meant they were a "degraded race." In a letter to one of his friends, he wrote that he thought three to four generations of Black people would have to die before they would be civilized enough to vote. It was, Armstrong maintained, "the duty of the superior white race to rule over the weaker dark-skinned races until they were appropriately civilized" by the moral power of labor and manual industry.

Armstrong's philosophy was strongly influenced by his father, Richard Armstrong. Samuel was born in 1839 in Maui, where his family had relocated to aid his father's missionary work. The elder Armstrong would later become superintendent of public instruction on the island, and in all the schools over which he presided, Indigenous students helped support the cost of their education by farming or working in blacksmithing and carpentry. For most of his teenage years, Samuel worked as his father's secretary and absorbed his views about Black and Indigenous students benefiting more from learning to work hard than from classical forms of education. When his father died, Armstrong left Hawaii for Massachusetts to attend Williams College. He graduated at the height of the Civil War and, along with many of his classmates, enthusiastically volunteered to join the fight. He fought and served with distinction at the Battle of Gettysburg, which earned him a promotion to major. He was twenty-five when he was appointed to lead the all-Black troop. By the end of the war, he had risen to the rank of brigadier general, and he was called General Armstrong the rest of his life.

In March 1866, a year after the war ended, Armstrong asked government officials to allow him to work to help educate and settle a group of newly freed Black people without homes who were camping out near Hampton, Virginia. The following year, he convinced the American Missionary Association to provide him with the funding to formalize the arrangement by opening a school. The school, named Hampton Normal and Agricultural Institute, opened its doors in 1868. As had been the case with Indigenous children who attended boarding schools and with those who attended the schools his father had run in Hawaii, students paid their school fees by doing work such as gardening and carpentry. Discipline in the school was vigorous, if not brutal. An investigator sent by the federal government to look in to complaints about the treatment of the students discovered that students were frequently sent to a "penal colony" a few miles from the main campus. There, students were sometimes enclosed in rooms without heat, air, or light, and without much food until adults determined they had been sufficiently chastised for whatever infraction of which they had been accused. Armstrong said this was necessary because the backbreaking work they did when enslaved had somehow "taught Black people to be lazy" and not take pride in their work. He also believed that because they were "pagans" back in Africa, they were a "degraded" people for whom harsh discipline was sometimes necessary.

Though originally conceived as a school that would only educate Black children, Armstrong began to educate Indigenous youth because the U.S. government was willing to pay him to do so. He also thought bringing in Indigenous children would help turn down the heat of the rising ire of white supremacists in Virginia, who had long been against the idea of educating Black children. In the aftermath of Nat Turner's slave rebellion in 1831, the Virginia legislature passed laws making it unlawful to teach the enslaved, free Black people, or biracial children to read or write. Similar laws were passed in other slave-holding states across the South. Though the Civil War rendered these laws moot, the sentiment and people who supported such restrictions remained and continued to intensify. Armstrong recognized a win-win proposition, and soon his twin missions became to "uplift" Black people from their state of "degradation" and to "civilize" the Indigenous "savage" and teach him to work. The funds the government provided him for the education of Indigenous children, along with charitable contributions, subsidized the education of the school's Black children, who received no such direct financial support.

One of the most recognizable graduates of Hampton was Booker T. Washington, who would rise to unprecedented levels of power and influence as the president of the Tuskegee Institute, one of the most successful HBCUs founded after the Civil War—an opportunity Armstrong arranged for him. But such accomplishments were despite and not because of Armstrong's views on Black and Indigenous people. Writing in 1888, Armstrong said, "You see I've only . . . boosted darkies a bit, and so to speak, lassoed wild Indians all to be cleaned and tame by a simple process I have invented known as the 'Hampton method.'"

Despite the income produced by educating Indigenous students, money remained an issue, and no matter how hard Armstrong tried to assuage their rage, the white citizens of Virginia who could grudgingly tolerate the idea of educating Indigenous children grew violently hostile to having Black students receive an education in their state. In addition, the commingling of children with different skin colors and cultures became a magnet for controversy. There were rumors that white and Black teachers might be sharing tables at the dining hall, and that Black and Indigenous students might be intermarrying or "mingling their blood" by having sexual relationships leading to children. Deep-seated beliefs about the dangers of educating Black children were so prevalent in the region that many Indigenous graduates reported being fired from jobs when employers learned they had attended a school with Black children. Not even the federal government's Indian Office would hire Indigenous Hampton grads. Hampton's program for Indigenous students ended in 1923 when Caroline Andrus, the program's director, resigned because she felt she could no longer prevent "amalgamation" between Indigenous and Black students. She wrote in 1923:

> Some of the other Indian girls flirted so with the colored boys that it made for a good deal of gossip of a kind I hate and despise. Now, there will probably be no Indian boys at the school this year and . . . I am afraid this sort of thing will be worse than before. The changed conditions made me feel I could no longer conscientiously bring children on from the West and that is the reason I resigned.

Along with segregated schools, this dizzyingly inventive opposition by white opponents to educating Black children proved to be among the grand themes in the story of Black education, crawling through the historical curtain from the nineteenth to the twentieth century. By 1896, codification of these practices was already happening. In the landmark *Plessy v. Ferguson* case, the U.S. Supreme Court declared forced segregation based on race constitutional. The attorney for Homer Plessy, who was suing the court over an 1892 incident in which he had refused to sit in a "Black only" railroad car, argued that racially separate public spaces, such as schools and public transportation, violated the government's responsibility to treat and protect all citizens equally. Plessy said his citizenship rights meant he was entitled to sit anywhere he pleased. But the Court rejected Plessy's argument, basically saying they were sorry he felt that way but simply did not agree that segregating races was a problem. A law that "implies merely a legal distinction" between white people and Black people, the justices argued, is not unconstitutional. "We consider the underlying fallacy of the plaintiff's argument to consist in the assumption that the enforced separation of the two races stamps the colored race with a badge of inferiority," the justices said in their decision. "If this be so, it is not by reason of anything found in the act, but solely because the colored race chooses to put that construction upon it." They determined that, so long as facilities were "separate but equal," racial segregation in and of itself was not problematic.

Of course, we know that facilities for Black people were rarely equal, and when even a glimmer of parity did surface—through sustained efforts by Black people—white supremacists were quick to squash it. Whether separate, unequal, barely existent, or just a promise, Black people in the South fervently sought out education and came to value learning and teaching above few other things. For Black communities in the South, a school was not just a building or a means to an economic end; it was access to the promises of mobility inherent in the American Dream and contained the potential for equality and citizenship. Yet as vehemently as they sought it out, so was it denied.

In a March 2001 *Washington Post* article, reporter Donald Baker chronicled one of the more extreme examples of white political resistance to integrated schools. The article tells the story of how white parents, politicians, and community members in Virginia's Prince Edward County so strongly resisted compliance with *Brown* that they chose to close every single public school to make sure none would be able to teach Black children. Shirley Davidson had been a one-year-old when the Supreme Court ruled in 1954 that southern schools, and by extension those across the country, should integrate. In 1959, Shirley was six years old and excited about beginning the first grade. But that was the year officials closed the entire public school system, and Shirley would be eleven before Black children in the county would once again be educated using public funds. Black children in the town lost five years of formal education. Officials used a variety of means to allow white children to continue to learn during this time, most notably opening white-only private schools, which were exempt from the *Brown* ruling, and giving white parents grants from public funds to pay for tuition. The grants provided one hundred dollars for each child from county funds and allowed taxpayers to donate up to 25 percent of their real and personal property taxes to a private school. Meanwhile, Black children like Shirley were completely shut out.

During the first few months of the shutdown, Shirley had remained hopeful. Each morning, she stood on her porch and watched the white neighborhood children board a school bus. Shirley so wanted to join them that each morning after they left, she grabbed a handful of books, plopped herself under a tree and daydreamed that one day a yellow school bus would take her to school, too. Some days, so caught up in her daydreams, she would still be sitting beneath the tree when the bus brought her white neighbors, Tommy and Billy, back home. Shirley's mother, Hazel, said she had not thought her daughter would be out of school for so long. She had, of course, heard of white people threatening to close schools to avoid integrating them, but she told the *Washington Post* reporter that she had paid little attention, because it seemed to her that they were always threatening to do something disturbing to demonstrate their superiority over Black people. She thought these were just empty words. But as the weeks rolled by and Black parents watched their children languish, Hazel said she and the other Black families came to understand what they were up against.

What Hazel did not know at the time was that the private schools, or "segregation academies," the white children in her county attended were part of a coordinated effort to evade integration called "Massive Resistance." According to the NAACP Legal Defense Fund, the high-level protest strategy conceived of by members of the U.S. Congress consisted of a series of laws that allowed southern states to take varied measures to prevent school integration, such as closing or withholding funding from integrated schools. In March 1956, South Carolina senator Strom Thurmond was first in drafting his vision for pushing back against the *Brown* ruling, quickly enlisting twenty senators and eighty-two members of the House of Representatives to his cause. In short order, the members supporting Massive Resistance included politicians from across the South, including Alabama, Arkansas, Georgia, Louisiana, Mississippi, South Carolina, and Virginia. Only three southern Democrats refused to sign: Albert Gore Sr., Estes Kefauver, and the future president Lyndon B. Johnson. The politicians, who referred to Thurmond's document as a manifesto, claimed their cause was justified, because the "original Constitution" did not mention education.

In September 1958, James Lindsay Almond Jr., who won Virginia's gubernatorial election by pledging to uphold Massive Resistance, closed schools in Charlottesville, Front Royal, and Norfolk rather than see Black children sit in classrooms with white children. By January 1959, both the federal and state supreme courts had overturned Massive Resistance laws and demanded that all closed schools be reopened. But local school officials in Prince Edward County rose up in defiance, and in March 1959 they closed all public schools in town. They kept them closed to Black children for five years, siphoning off the public funds earmarked for all public schools and using the money to open a white-only privately run "academy." This allowed white parents to continue to educate their children while evading the *Brown* decision and excluding Black children from taxpayer-supported schools.

With the precedent set, segregation academies and the unequal system they espoused took hold across the South in the decades following *Brown v. Board of Education*. Sometimes referred to as "Freedom of Choice Schools," segregation academies were founded in Mississippi in the mid-1950s by a white supremacist group known as the White Citizens Council. Based on the "free market" ideas of University of Chicago economist Milton Friedman, the schools were conceived of as a legal way to work around the *Brown* decision, which excluded private schools. These academies flourished throughout the 1960s and 1970s, with southern state legislatures freely allowing white parents to use taxpayer dollars to finance their children's education. In Mississippi, lawmakers provided white parents with vouchers of up to $240, which, depending on the tuition charged, could pay for between 50 and 90 percent of their children's white-only, private school educations. Predictably, they did not often provide the same for Black parents. In 1969, of the forty-nine schools receiving state-provided tuition vouchers in Mississippi, forty-eight were white-only segregation academies. These funding schemes were so successful that by 1970, roughly 300,000 students were enrolled in all-white private schools across eleven southern states, and by 1974, that number rose to 750,000 white children enrolled across 3,500 academies.

At the same time, white enrollment in public schools declined precipitously. In Jackson, Mississippi, alone it fell by twelve thousand students, going from representing more than half of the student body in 1969 to less than a third in 1976. The resulting demographic shift caused a drastic reduction in the funds available to educate the predominantly Black children left behind in the public school system, as tax dollars earmarked for them followed white children both to these quasi-private academies and to public schools that, operating with impunity well into the 1970s, remained segregated.

Officials in Prince Edward County, where little Shirley lived, were singular in their defiance of court orders—waging a resistance so long and merciless that it inflicted economic and psychological suffering for generations. Public schools in Prince Edward County remained closed until 1964. With 90 percent of white children being educated in white-only segregation academies during the period when public schools were shut down, white officials were in no great rush to figure out a solution for the education of Black children.

As word of the district-wide school closings in Prince Edward

County spread, individuals and organizations came to the little town of Farmville and others throughout the county to help displaced Black children learn. One of the most active organizations was the American Friends Service Committee, the social service branch of the Quakers, which sent people to help local Black ministers and the NAACP in setting up "freedom schools." Many unemployed Black teachers were hired as instructors, holding classes in the basements of Black churches throughout the county. The idea was to keep the children from falling too far behind during what almost everyone believed would be a short period. They thought things would get back to normal once their white neighbors and community tired of showing their power. They miscalculated.

As the *Washington Post* article recounts, by midsummer 1960, it became clear that schools would remain closed for a second year. Alarmed about what was going to happen to the locked-out Black children, Quaker social worker Jean Fairfax began calling friends and contacts across the country, asking them to house students so they could attend schools outside the state. Seventy Black children packed their bags and left their homes for regions all over the nation. One, a young man named James E. Ghee Jr., landed in Iowa City with the family of a University of Iowa economics professor whose wife, a Japanese American, had survived internment at a relocation camp during World War II. She, too, had been rescued by Quakers, who had sent her to live with a family in Chicago. She told the reporter that she saw taking in a Prince Edward child as a chance to karmically repay the debt. Another displaced student named Moses Scott was taken in by a family who lived in the Boston suburb of Newton. There, he stayed with a Jewish family in which both parents were Holocaust survivors. Prince Edward students ended up all over the Midwest and the East Coast.

More children could have been placed, but many Black parents refused to let white supremacy separate them from their children. During the first few months of the system shutdown, when spirit and resolve were highest, most children remained in Farmville—optimistic that the winds would soon shift. The Quaker-run Freedom Schools in Prince Edward County enrolled only about 650 pupils, hamstrung by a lack of credentialed teachers, money to pay them, and adequate space. This was just about one-third of the 1,700 displaced Black students. Several hundred others commuted to schools in surrounding counties or were sent to live with relatives out of state. The situation worsened when Black teachers found jobs elsewhere, leaving even fewer qualified people in the area willing to teach Black children for free.

Carlton Terry was twelve the year Prince Edward County schools closed to Black children. Thinking back on that first year, he said, "All I knew was that I wasn't in school, and I knew the reason why. I realized that the legal system was not working, at least not working for me. I remember sitting at home, watching Amos 'n' Andy on TV, shell-shocked. I read the newspaper every day to see what would happen." After a year sitting at home, his family, as was true for most Black families, came to understand there was no real end in sight. They decided to take the Quakers up on their offer to send him to school in Massachusetts. In reflecting on the period, he says, "I only lost one year, and I feel like I was hurt. But imagine what it must be like for those who lost four or five years, or never went back." By the spring of 1960, a federal judge again ruled that Virginia had to stop using taxpayer money to fund a school system only for white children. No matter—at least initially, district officials ignored that court ruling. In addition, white officials helped themselves to public school resources, simply taking what they wanted from locked public schools. They took books, desks, and even goalposts for a new football field at the private, white-only school. A local businessman, Robert Taylor, recalled that white officials took "everything but the clocks." Carlton Terry, the young man who had to relocate to Massachusetts to receive an education, told the *Washington Post* reporter that he "eventually got to the point where I hated whites."

For the first few years, the federal government ignored the continued

Massive Resistance taking place in plain view. President Dwight Eisenhower, who was in office from 1953 to 1961, was no fan of *Brown*, once noting that it was unlikely white people would comply with the ruling. "I do not believe that prejudices," he said, "will succumb to compulsion," adding that he believed imposing federal law on the states "would set back the cause of race relations a long, long time." Initially, pleas to Eisenhower about this slow murder of children's educational futures did not garner much response at all. It took until Christmas of 1962, three years into the standoff, for the Justice Department to join the NAACP as a friend of the court in its appeal of the Prince Edward case. By then, the nation had a new presidential administration and a new attorney general named Robert F. Kennedy. He joined the fray, filing a legal brief arguing that states' rights aside, federal courts retained the power to require the Virginia county to levy taxes that would be used to operate desegregated public schools. Then, in a special message to Congress on civil rights in February 1963, the attorney general's brother, President John Kennedy, urged the parties to reach a speedy resolution of the legal issues and promised aid for the remedial education of Black children when the schools reopened. He pledged to "fulfill the constitutional objective of an equal, non-segregated educational opportunity for all children." Speaking on the centennial of the Emancipation Proclamation, Robert Kennedy noted "with as much sadness as irony that outside of Africa south of the Sahara, the only places on earth known not to provide free public education are Communist China, North Vietnam, Sarawak [Borneo], British Honduras—and Prince Edward County."

The brothers continued to apply pressure. More than just offering talk, Kennedy's administration joined state and private organizers in creating a new entity called the Prince Edward County Free School Association and rented three of the closed public schools for Black students to attend during the 1963–64 school year. School and other elected officials were still unwilling to desegregate, fund, and reopen all public schools, so foundations, businesses, and individuals from around the country took up the mantle, contributing a total of $1 million to help provide accredited, robust educational offerings to Black students in this unorthodox fashion. Neil Sullivan, a principal in a Long Island school district, took leave from his job to run one of the schools, called the Prince Edward County Free School. Sullivan sought out and hired a multiracial faculty from around the country to teach at the school. In the spring of 1964, Robert Kennedy and his wife, Ethel, visited Farmville to assess these privately funded experimental Free (as opposed to public) Schools that had come into being under his leadership. Two weeks after their visit, and ten years after the *Brown* decision, the U.S. Supreme Court ordered Prince Edward County to reopen and desegregate its schools, and the district finally felt forced to comply.

By then, Prince Edward Academy was the only segregation academy that remained open in the state, and its operators rushed to plunder more educational dollars from the taxpayer coffers before the deadline. The summer before the public schools were set to open, white administrators set aside $180,000 meant to go toward the schools that the county's 1,700 Black children would finally be allowed to attend. But at the same time, on that same day in July, they approved a law to allocate that exact amount of money in grants to white parents who wanted to continue to send their children to the white-only private school. Anticipating that a federal judge would issue an injunction to block the illegal plan, the town officials instructed the seven hundred white parents of academy students to gather at the school board at two a.m. if they wanted to receive one last tuition grant. There, the board gave the waiting parents $250 grants on a first-come, first-served basis, until the grant funds were exhausted, for a total of $180,000. With checks in hand, the lucky academy parents rushed to one of the town's three banks, which had opened early so the recipients could deposit their checks before a new court order could stop them. The bit of justice found in this story is that two years later, a federal appeals court ruled that the six county officials on the Board of Supervisors who had approved both the scheme and its unorthodox timing were personally responsible for repaying the funds to the county.

On September 16, 1963, a full four years after the public schools had been padlocked, Shirley Davidson finally got to ride a school bus. She was among 1,520 students, all but four of whom were Black, who enrolled in the Free School system the Kennedy administration had helped open. Black children had schools, but after all that time, money, heartbreak, separation, and tragedy, it was still segregated and, because of the white officials' scheme, still did not have access to taxpayer funds. During the years she had been out of school, Hazel had tutored her daughter Shirley in reading and math, so when schools opened, Shirley was well prepared academically. The same was far from true for the majority. Neil Sullivan confidently announced in the press that "our first task will be a mass attack on reading skills," but he confided to an interviewer that "four years' loss will never be made up entirely." A student named Sylvia Eanes was in the third grade when the schools were closed. She said she was placed in the eighth grade when they reopened, as though she had been in school all along. She recalled, "The teachers just pushed us through, wanted us out."

After graduation, Sylvia didn't think she could spell well enough to pass the test to fulfill her dream of one day becoming a licensed practical nurse. She settled for a job in a local food-processing factory. Her older brother, McCarthy, drove a school bus for white children during the closings. He was twenty-one when he returned to school and twenty-two when he graduated, was drafted, and sent to Vietnam. When asked to reflect on the time, he told the reporter for the *Washington Post,* "My country called me to fight in Vietnam, but wouldn't let me go to school." It was not until 1978 that the last school district to have used public money to support private white schools ceased to do so. In the 1940s and 1950s, we in the United States were told by psychologists, lawyers, and civil rights leaders that integration was the cure for the chronic underemployment, low college completion rates, and economic disparities faced by Black and other economically and politically vulnerable people. No one warned about how the cost, extreme white backlash, could further harm Black children who just wanted to learn. The problems were not confined to the South.

In the decade or so after *Brown*, Black people in the United States had reason to believe that at last the equal citizenship they had long fought for might be coming into view. Several events, aside from the Supreme Court deeming them worthy of equality in classrooms, promised a new phase in the Black freedom struggle: starting in December 1955, the yearlong Montgomery Bus Boycott, which saw tens of thousands of Black people in Montgomery, Alabama, refusing to ride the city's buses to protest segregation and maltreatment, had brought a twenty-seven-year-old preacher named Martin Luther King and a longtime activist named Rosa Parks onto the world stage. The Civil Rights Act passed in 1964, striking down Jim Crow laws and prohibiting discrimination based on race. But by 1968, government reports told a story of urban cities with education systems so bad that young Black people were inspired to rage in rebellion. Once-strong school systems in cities like Detroit, Baltimore, Chicago, Newark, and elsewhere wobbled as white families fled to the suburbs, leaving behind poorly staffed and funded institutions that, because the troubles were blamed on poor or nonexistent Black family structures, damaged and overpoliced the Black children left behind in them.

Because racial segregation was not written into law in the North, most of its school districts, courts, and politicians claimed that the *Brown* decision did not apply to them. Whatever segregation did exist, lawyers and politicians argued, was a natural byproduct of racist discrimination in housing rather than an issue within schools themselves. This de facto segregation, though damaging to the prospects of societal advancement for American citizens who were poor and of color, was legal, they said. Of course, the NAACP argued that the *Brown* decision should apply to de facto segregation as well, and civil rights groups sued school boards in cities such as Cincinnati, Ohio; Detroit, Michigan; Richmond, California; and Boston, Massachusetts, among others, urging school districts to integrate. But in the 1960s North, rising levels of anti-integration activism, not courtroom battles, most forcefully brought the issues of race, segregation, and education to a head. Though the South receives the lion's share of focus regarding the pushback against integration, white rejection of Black children in white schools above the Mason-Dixon Line was no less ugly.

New York City is but one city where there was concern among citizens and elected officials alike about the *Brown* decision. While there were certainly some who wanted New York to get a jump on desegregating schools, others had already actively started plotting for the opposite. In 1964, the New York City Board of Education proposed a plan that would have seen a modest forty thousand of the one million students enrolled in the district transferred to different schools through a combination of school rezoning and busing. White people who opposed mandatory integration decrees protested against sending their children to schools outside their neighborhoods, but their true concerns were revealed in their rejection of a plan that would do the opposite: bus Black and Latino students between Harlem and predominantly white Staten Island. The protesters were so vocal and vigorous in their resistance to the city's desegregation plans that school officials soon completely abandoned any efforts to either integrate or desegregate schools in the city. Today, New York City schools are the most segregated in the nation.

According to research by the historian Matt Delmont, Black parents and civil rights advocates, like seasoned activist Ella Baker and sociologist Kenneth Clark—whose research with his wife, Mamie, was central to the *Brown* decision—urged city officials to institute desegregation plans. In 1964, in one of the largest civil rights protests to have taken place in the United States, Reverend Milton Galamison organized a citywide boycott of New York City schools through an organization called the Citywide Committee for Integrated Schools. The boycott was also supported by the NAACP, the Congress of Racial Equality, the National Urban League, the Harlem Parents' Committee, and the Parents' Workshop for Equality. On the day, 460,000 students and teachers stayed out of school to protest the lack of a comprehensive plan for desegregation, marching through the city to bring attention to the fact that racial segregation was not confined to the South. In the decade between the *Brown* decision and the boycott, march leaders pointed out, segregation in New York City schools had become more entrenched rather than dissipating. Pleased with the initial turnout, organizers planned a second boycott for the following month. But before the second march could take place, thousands of white parents—mostly white mothers—marched in slush and snow across the Brooklyn Bridge in counterprotest. As they walked, they came up with little songs and chants that all had one thing in common: they were against any integration plans that involved busing their children into schools in the city's "slums." Their objections made clear that the fight for integration was held back by the view that majority-Black schools were inherently flawed and degraded by having Black children in classrooms with other Black children. In 1963, according to a *New York Times* article, the state's education commissioner, Dr. James E. Allen Jr., warned that "any school that exceeds a non-white enrollment of 50 per cent is 'in danger' of becoming racially imbalanced—with the implication that such imbalance is equivalent with inferior education." In school districts outside the South, the desire to implement desegregation kept coming up against white people's unwillingness to accept any changes. This would become an enduring theme with significant national consequences.

Even integration supporters were divided in their views on the best way forward, with some calling for immediate and total integration and others preferring a slower, more deliberate approach. In a 1964 *New York Times* article covering the boycott and these conflicting views, a reporter observed that the "big city school systems face the threat of a serious split—not between integrationists and segregationists but between civil rights leaders who are asking for total and instant integration of the schools and those who have long been working for a combination of school improvement and integration but are afraid that extreme and impractical steps may destroy the school system." According to the article, those who did not believe in forced integration warned that if white children were "shipped against their parents' will into schools deep inside slum areas, the consequence will be an exodus of white, middle-class families, either into the suburbs or into private schools." This, they feared, "would make the racial imbalance even more unfavorable." The answer, then, was to place the burden of desegregating white suburban schools on Black children.

In Boston, at least initially, school officials refused to acknowledge racial segregation was an issue in their schools. Massachusetts was, after all, the state where the first law prohibiting segregated schools was passed in 1855. Perhaps not surprisingly, the law was rarely enforced in practice. More than one hundred years after it was established, in 1963, the city's NAACP branch finally won a case that led to the creation of a program that hoped to make concrete the promises of desegregation. Operation Exodus was a busing plan funded by private donations to redistribute Black children in Boston's high-poverty Roxbury area to wealthier schools in greater Boston. And though it was praised by activists and the press, it did not lead to Boston Public Schools admitting to the existence of racial disparities in their school system or to its responsibility for fixing it. It wasn't until 1965 that the state legislature passed a bill both acknowledging the issue and proposing ways to remedy it. The Racial Imbalance Act authorized the state to withhold funds from any public school district deemed to be perpetuating "racial imbalance," which, though there was no language like this in the *Brown* decision, legislators defined as schools having more than 50 percent of non-white students. It also enabled city and town school committees and districts to help alleviate "racial isolation" (defined as any public school where over 70 percent of the student population was Black) through *voluntary* cross-district enrollment. No one who did not want to would be forced to participate. It is worth noting that, because the act's definition of racial imbalance did not apply to majority-white schools, the onus of desegregation fell on non-white rather than white students. Given that white people were the ones weaponizing segregation to their benefit, this decision facilitated continued resistance to integration, leaving non-white students to bear the brunt of busing programs. More Black students would end up in white, wealthier schools, yes, but the lack of reciprocal busing meant the schools they left behind would not benefit from the resources and benefits white students attract.

Still, organizations and groups in the Boston suburbs, such as fair housing advocates, civil rights committees, churches, and members of school boards, saw the moment as one that might lead to change and began to strategize about how to enroll Black students in better-resourced schools under the Racial Imbalance Act. One group presented what they called the Metropolitan Council for Educational Opportunity (METCO), which would become the longest-running and most successful voluntary school integration program in the country. Started in 1966, METCO bused thousands of students from predominantly Black and Latino neighborhoods in the city of Boston, and later Springfield, to white, wealthy neighborhoods in the suburbs. Its founders assumed the program would be temporary, hoping that housing segregation would dissipate over time, and that schools would naturally come to educate Black and white children alongside one another without the need for yellow buses. But the program continues to this day.

Despite its lofty goals and even support in some white suburban communities, METCO was criticized from the start. Alana Semuels, a participant in the program in the 1980s, wrote in a 2011 article in *The*

Atlantic that some questioned the program's emphasis on modest racial integration in the suburbs, as opposed to in Boston itself. This strategy, some observed, did not solve the problem of racially segregated schools, helping a relatively small number of Black students while leaving the majority behind. And many urban working-class whites viewed METCO as perpetuating a form of reverse racism because of its emphasis on Black and non-white children—a focus they viewed as discriminatory against their own children, who were also left behind in underperforming and underfunded city schools.

Those views aside, students able to participate in the program had high graduation rates and attained graduate degrees at levels comparable to white students in the district. What METCO showed was that if the numbers were kept relatively small, and if it did not inconvenience white families, desegregating white suburban schools with Black urban children could work for at least a few. This success came at a cost: many Black alumni of the program have written and spoken about the traumatic impacts of long bus rides, racial aggressions, slurs, assaults, and the lack of teachers of color to serve as role models. Despite those drawbacks, the successful aspects of the program led other cities to try to replicate it.

But consistent pushback from suburban school districts who resisted the calls of urban Black people to open their schools to desegregation efforts led to the matter ending up before the Supreme Court. There, the effort to force suburban communities to participate in school desegregation programs was rebuffed by the Supreme Court in yet another landmark case regarding the education of Black children in the United States. It was called *Milliken v. Bradley* and brought the Midwest into the national conversation about how to equitably educate Black children in public schools when white families did not want them.

In Detroit, like in many places across the country, desegregation efforts dragged into the 1970s. Responding to the considerable

legal and community pressure to at least try to comply with *Brown,*
the school board proposed a redrawing of boundary lines to make
schools as racially and economically integrated as possible. But before
this redistricting could take effect, the majority-white state legislature stepped in and killed the plan. In response, in August 1970, the
NAACP filed a lawsuit against state officials, including Governor William Milliken, arguing that although schools were not officially segregated by race as a matter of state policy, the city of Detroit and the
state had allowed suburbs to build figurative but strong walls to shut
out Black children. These policy walls, they argued, thwarted integration polices and increased racial segregation in city schools. Tensions
were so high around the issue of school integration that, a few months
before the NAACP filed their suit, Ku Klux Klan members blew up
ten school buses in the Detroit suburb of Pontiac rather than let them
be used to bus students to white schools.

The district court judge who heard the NAACP's argument,
Stephen Roth, tried to hold the state and legislature responsible for
segregation, ordering the city of Detroit—which was by then almost
completely Black due to white families leaving in large numbers for
the suburbs—to participate in a regional busing plan between cities
and suburbs. But the state appealed the decision, eventually bringing
the case to the Supreme Court. The court took up the case in February
1974 and struck down the lawsuit 5–4, saying that since the suburbs
did not cause Detroit's problems, suburbanites did not have to be part
of the solution. The *Milliken* case absolved white parents of any responsibility for integration and effectively halted a strategy that would have
helped Detroit achieve desegregation and given Black children access
to the well-resourced schools white people had established in its suburbs. Joyce Baugh, a professor who has written extensively about the
case, says it intensified white people's desire to "move away from urban
schools to, in effect, outrun desegregation."

Ultimately, the concerns of New York City activists who feared that a forced approach to integration would cause white people to leave the city proved to be true in some places. A report released in May 1968 by the National Advisory Commission on Civil Disorders, known as the Kerner Commission, identified the migration of white people out of urban areas as a core impediment to integration, because it left a racial imbalance in city schools that would not be easily reversed. "No matter how great the effort toward desegregation, many children of the ghetto will not, within their school careers, attend integrated schools," the report read. In some cities, most notably Boston, New York, Chicago, and Philadelphia, elected officials were able to promise and deliver white parents a level of racial segregation in city schools that kept the majority from decamping to the suburbs. In other cities, like Detroit, Baltimore, Newark, and St. Louis, by the mid-1960s white people were moving their families in increasingly large numbers to predominantly white suburbs and out of reach of school desegregation efforts. Termed "white flight," this mass migration from cities to suburbs was as influential on the trajectory of Black education as was the *Brown* decision. Desegregation simply could not happen if there were no white children available in metropolitan areas to attend urban schools.

The Kerner Commission, an eleven-member bipartisan body headed by Illinois governor Otto Kerner, was formed by President Lyndon Johnson to investigate the surge of violent uprisings that had engulfed American cities over the previous few years. The president, in his charge to the commission, said he wanted to know the following: "What happened? Why did it happen? What can be done to prevent it from happening again and again?" The resulting report clocked in at over seven hundred pages. After identifying and analyzing more than 150 incidents of unrest between 1965 and 1968, the commission said that though many, such as the powerful FBI director J. Edgar Hoover, believed the violence a result of the rising tide of Black militancy, their findings made clear that "white racism" was in fact to blame. In what would become its most memorable line, the report asserted that "our nation is moving toward two societies, one Black, one white—separate and unequal." It called for expanded aid to foster greater educational, economic, and employment options and outcomes for urban Black communities as a means of preventing further violence.

The commission identified failing schools as one of the most persistent sources of grievance and resentment in urban Black communities, noting that these sentiments fueled urban uprisings. "The hostility of Negro parents and students toward the school system is generating increasing conflict and causing disruption," the report read, noting a high incidence of riot participation "by ghetto youth who have not completed high school." It offered a sobering assessment, concluding that "Negro students are falling further behind whites with each year of school completed" and pointing to the underemployment rate among Black youth as "evidence, in part, of the growing educational crisis." As commission members traveled across the urban North conducting interviews, they found that for white and wealthy students, the schools "discharged their responsibilities well." Children attending schools in "urban ghettos" across the whole of the country, however, were not as well served. These schools, the report said, "have failed to provide the educational experiences which could overcome the effects of discrimination and deprivation." Having diagnosed the extent of the educational malady, the commission offered a tentative treatment plan, arguing that a democratic society "must equip children to develop their potential to participate fully in American life." In an endorsement of racial integration, including in schools, the report said that "it is indispensable that opportunities for interaction between the races be expanded." In theory, schools offer such opportunities for interaction. But too often, across the United States, Black children have been barred outside the doors of welcome.

In thinking about how the resistance to equally educating Black children spanned the South and the North, it is worth mentioning

that, after a former governor of Alabama, George Wallace, stood in
the doorway of a University of Alabama building in 1963 and declared
"Segregation today, Segregation tomorrow, Segregation Forever,"
he received more than one hundred thousand telegrams, 95 percent
of which were supportive of his actions. More than half came from
outside the South. Receiving the telegrams was a revelation for him.
"They all hate black people, all of them. They're all afraid, all of them.
Great God! That's it! They're all Southern! The whole United States is
Southern!" Wallace told NBC News reporter Douglas Kiker in 1968.
Given this history, I believe that though many view *Brown v. Board* as
a significant civil rights–era win, it led to what Kiese Laymon refers
to in his award-winning memoir, *Heavy,* as "unacknowledged scars
from battles won, that hurt more than battles lost." On the other side
of this white resistance to having Black children in white schools were
the Black teachers, schools, and communities who wanted and knew
how to educate them. My grandparents, Milton and Evelyn, were in
this group.

BLACK TEACHERS MATTER

In the 1950s, Clearwater Heights in Pinellas County, Florida, was a thriving Black community, with roads made from packed, red-tinged dirt that was cool on bare feet. It felt pleasant—nothing like the discomfort of the waves of heat that radiate from the gray asphalt roads the city laid in the 1970s. At mid-century, pictures show wide streets lined with modest homes owned by Black service workers, teachers, and beauticians. There were at least three small, one-room churches built on ground the Black congregations owned. Abutting the houses of worship were cemeteries where members of the segregated Black community laid their loved ones to rest.

In 1951, the city of Clearwater decided to move two different "Negro" cemeteries to make way for a swimming pool, a department store, and a Black school. Only later was it revealed that the bodies buried underneath the ground were never removed. A former gravedigger turned funeral home operator named O'Neal Larkin was eighty-two when, in 2022, he told a journalist that he watched a construction crew cut through two coffins when digging a trench through the supposedly empty property. The gravedigger said his employers told him and his fellow Black workers to dig for bodies only if there were headstones marking the graves. Larkin said he had always known that not all the families could afford such expenditures. He was sure more bodies remained behind.

The Black community where Larkin plied his trade has since been displaced by gentrification, high taxes, and the discovery that the land on which the community sat was illegally fouled by discarded toxic chemicals used in agriculture and manufacturing to the point of being dangerous to human beings. I recall my father telling me in the 1980s that the neighborhood had been declared a Superfund site, which made it eligible for infusions of cash from the federal government for the cleanup and removal of the toxins. By then, there were few community members left to remember that county officials who bought the land had promised to move the bodies or that, when questioned, they had assured family members that "their people" had been dug up and reburied across town.

When I was a child in the 1970s, I played in the ruins of Williams Elementary, the school that had been built atop the old cemetery. It had been closed for over a decade by then, and little more than crumble and decay remained. When I look at the yearbook photos of it during its heyday, I see orderly rows of desks, grinning children, a clean cafeteria, artwork, smiling children or stern-faced teachers, janitors, and administrative staff. It is hard to square these images with the space I wandered through a full decade after it was closed and left to rot. There were desks, yes, but they were hobbled and overturned. There were books and blackboards, sure, but the books were home to bugs and yellowed pages stuck so tightly together by mildew, dirt, and water that there were often few visible words worth trying to read. The blackboards were as often in pieces on the floor as affixed to a wall. Many seemed to have exploded, littering the concrete floor. If I cut through our backyard to get there, the school stood a short half a block from the house I shared with my grandparents. One day, even its carcass disappeared, leaving empty land, haunted as much by what lay below as by what had stood above. I sometimes wonder if I am drawn to think, talk, and write about what segregation built and desegregation dismantled because of the specter of my youthful communion with a ruin where past and present, living and dead, collided.

I was in college when my grandmother told me she had taught at that school for decades, and that my grandfather had been a social science teacher who had also presided over the political science club, where he guided students in understanding how and why the politics of the past and present mattered. My grandmother excelled at teaching reading, helping children who had been alive for less than a decade unravel the riddle of letters and learn how these fit together to make words. I can still picture her when she first started to talk about Williams, our family, and the Black people who lived in Clearwater: head bowed, hands in lap, swallowed by the size of the black plastic chair that pushed back into something approximating a bed. But what caught my attention, made me focus and hold my breath for a beat longer than its comfortable rhythm, was the little shrug she made with one of her shoulders and the small shake of her head as she whispered, "We lost it. We didn't know." She was talking about the school and the educational community it had fostered, which had meant so much to her.

She would never tell me much at once, but over time, as we watered vegetables, snapped peas, set up tables for bridge parties, or went to visit her sister, my aunt Mary, she told me stories about the school. Her memories tumbled forth in pieces that started down paths unfamiliar to me, leading to a world I didn't know and giving a different kind of meaning to the lives of the adults I had seen my whole life but knew so little about. My uncle, Shirley Curtis, was not just a silent, cigar-smoking man with few words for anyone as he sat hour after hour on his front porch. He had been a teacher, an educational leader, and a writer who had edited a newsletter for Black teachers in the segregated South and had a Black elementary school named after him to commemorate his efforts. My grandmother's favored bridge partner,

Mrs. Hodges, who always matched her handbag with her shoes and earrings in ways that pulled the whole together, had also been a teacher.

At the time, my grandmother's stories were interesting, but I didn't understand them in the way that I do now. These people had once viewed themselves as communally raising and protecting Black children. By the time the *Brown v. Board* case had been decided, almost 80 percent of Black teachers in Florida were also members of the NAACP, and some, like my grandfather, Milton Rooks Sr., were part of the group's leadership at a time when state legislators would harass, terrorize, and fire Black people who admitted the relationship. Over time, after my grandmother had a stroke that made it hard for her to string her words together in ways others could understand, and to fill in the silences between us when we would be driving around, fishing, or just spending too much silent time together, I started asking my father questions about Williams Elementary and Pinellas High, which he had attended. His stories and memories were almost never about the classes, outings, parties, or sporting events in which he and his classmates participated. Instead, he often talked about the vision of Black education his parents instilled in him and the adults who had taught him to see Black education as holistically tied to Black power, freedom, and self-determination. As an adult, I was able to find the activists he mentioned in books and archives. They were all teachers. They were all political leaders.

One of my grandparents' friends, Harry Moore, founded the first NAACP chapter in the state of Florida in the early 1930s and served for a time as its president. My grandfather served in the executive leadership of the Pinellas County chapter from the mid-1940s until the mid-1950s, when the *Brown* decision was handed down. Over a fifteen-year period, he and another friend, Noah Griffin, served in various roles in the chapter, including swapping terms as president. The three men also held leadership positions in the Florida State Teachers Association, an advocacy group that represented Black teachers in pay equity cases and supported those who were harassed or fired from their jobs for demanding equality in treatment, pay, and resources. Together, the men founded another statewide organization called the Progressive Voters League. Its purpose was to collaborate with Black teachers in organizing their communities to elect politicians dedicated to easing Black suffering and holding white politicians accountable to Black issues and concerns. Before settling in Florida, Mr. Griffin had taught for a time at the historically Black Lincoln University, where he developed a lifelong friendship with one of his prize students, a young man named Thurgood Marshall. While Mr. Marshall came to be most widely known as the lawyer who argued for and won the *Brown* decision and, later, the first Black person appointed to the Supreme Court, earlier in his career he represented Black teachers fighting for equal pay and treatment. These teachers thought little about integration as an ideal or goal; they were fighting to live more equally within segregated Black communities. As a result, before the idea of integration became the law of the land, the vision Black teachers had for Black freedom was for southern states to abide by the "separate but equal" mandate, pushing state governments to pay Black teachers salaries equal to those paid to whites. Like-minded Black teacher organizations in Maryland, Georgia, and Alabama embraced the strategy, and, at least initially, this plan bore fruit. Between 1939 and 1947, with the help of Thurgood Marshall and the NAACP, Black teachers won twenty-seven out of thirty-one salary equalization cases. However, despite the early wins, progress was agonizingly slow or sabotaged, as southern states, rather than comply with the judgments in favor of Black plaintiffs, simply fired them.

My grandmother, along with Harry Moore, the NAACP chapter founder, and his wife, Harriette, learned the roots of their philosophy on Black education at the same place, though at different times: on the Bethune-Cookman University campus. Founded by a woman named Mary McLeod Bethune, the college pushed back against white supremacy and its declaration of Black inferiority with an educational philosophy that wove together education, entrepreneurship, mutual aid, and electoral politics. Bethune's school trained Black teachers in what was called the Lab School, where Black children from the surrounding community came to learn. She opened a hospital so Black women students at her school could train to become nurses. Bethune helped prospective teachers see themselves as freedom fighters whose superpowers were literacy, organizing, and securing voting rights to make Black people safe and empower them to stand tall and strong in the warmth of their communal sun. When Noah and Terressa Griffin were fired from their jobs as teachers in segregated schools in Pinellas County for filing pay equity suits, the Black-owned Central Insurance Agency, founded by Bethune, helped pay Griffin a salary in acknowledgment of the sacrifice he made on behalf of the hope for Black equality. Bethune believed reading and writing were important parts of education, but knew character and courage were also key and taught these lessons to students like Harry and Harriette in the 1930s, and my grandmother in the late 1940s.

In 1920, these intertwined priorities played out on the Bethune-Cookman campus after state officials put a law on the books requiring Black people to prove they were literate before they could vote. Teachers at Bethune-Cookman conducted night classes to teach reading to adults. These classes led to threats from members of the white community, who did not want Black people to vote. One evening, the Ku Klux Klan warned Bethune that if she and the teachers at her school didn't stop teaching reading, they would come to the school and destroy it. The night of their arrival, city officials turned off the streetlamps in the town so that when the Klan members rode onto the campus on horseback, they were illuminated only by the orange-tinted flicker of their burning torches. As the caravan approached, Bethune instructed the staff to turn on lights in all the school buildings. When the Klan arrived, they found the campus completely lit up. Their group of eighty was dwarfed by the one hundred and fifty students, staff, and teachers who stood beside Bethune singing "God Will Take Care of You." This solidarity reflects the holistic vision of Black education Bethune's students were taught, where dignity, courage, intellect, and community were parts of a necessary whole.

These Black teachers did not see themselves as just teaching music, reading, or science, but also as activists, organizers, and freedom fighters who dreamed of and fought for an equitable world for future generations. Teaching was also a practice in strengthening community and a way to show Black children how to fight for respect and societal change. Talking with my grandmother, I learned Williams Elementary closed in 1965 because it was full of Black children, teachers, administrators, and staff. My grandmother didn't say it quite like that, but what she meant is that, after the *Brown v. Board* decision, instead of contemplating productive ways to blend what had been two separate school systems, local white officials chose instead to fire Black teachers and to close Black schools. She was the first person to explain to me that the price of equal citizenship for Black people, in what was for her the future, was the loss of her job, her husband's job, and the jobs of most of their friends who also worked in the segregated school system. My grandparents were not unique in this experience. The former dean of Howard University's School of Education, Leslie Fenwick, estimates the total number of Black teachers and principals fired following the *Brown* decision to have been roughly one hundred thousand and the economic impact on Black communities due to the loss of salaries as equivalent to roughly $2.2 billion today. Black teachers like my grandparents, Milton and Evelyn, had worried and warned this might be the case. They were proud of their schools and teachers and feared that the implementation of the *Brown* decision would sever community bonds and jeopardize their sense of self-determination.

We do not often talk about southern public schoolteachers in the 1930s, '40s, and '50s in relation to Black Power, but we should. It was a Black teacher who supported the Black youth activism that resulted in one of the five cases that became *Brown v. Board*—the only one of the five that was the result of student activism. In that case, a teenager named Barbara Johns helped organize and lead a two-week-long strike in which 450 of her classmates participated. They were mentored by a music teacher named Inez Davenport, who gave them the opportunity to talk about how they felt attending classes in schools with leaky roofs, rickety furnishings, a lack of indoor plumbing, and cast-off textbooks from white schools. The white students attended a new high school, replete with science labs, indoor plumbing, steam heat, a gym, and a well-stocked library. One day in the fall of 1950, when her students were complaining about the miserable state of their school, Davenport shared a news article with them about some Massachusetts students who had gone on strike and won their requested concessions. She told her students, "If they could do that, so could you."

After Davenport shared the news article, Barbara stayed after class to talk to her teacher. She said she knew that strikes brought some American workers better wages, but she had never imagined that students could strike, too. That afternoon's exchange was the beginning of a secret student-teacher collaboration. Davenport's urging was straightforward. She told Barbara, "If the kids went on strike, the school board would get the message—these kids are serious; let's build them a better school." But she also knew that a strike could put her own and perhaps others' jobs at risk. She told Barbara that they could no longer be seen talking one-on-one. They must communicate in writing, through notes placed in a music book on Davenport's desk. They destroyed the notes after reading them. Absolute secrecy was essential, Davenport insisted. As was so often the case with Black activist teachers at the time, Davenport was immediately fired once the initial lawsuit was filed. Her husband, the principal at the school, was fired as well.

Black teachers were not just dedicated to the education of children in the segregated south, but more broadly to civil rights, Black humanity, and an ethic of caring, justice, and the mobilization of Black people to fight for their citizenship rights. They believed self-knowledge, including Black history, and communal pride, along with the presence of Black leaders and caring teachers, were the building blocks for Black safety and protection for children and adults alike. In this regard, there were few teachers as important in the south as Harry Moore.

From 1927 to 1936, Moore was first a teacher, and then became principal of Titusville Colored Junior High School in Brevard, Florida. His wife, Harriette, was sometimes a teacher and sometimes a lunch lady at various elementary schools in the area. Troubled by the inequities and lack of educational resources available to Black children, Moore started the Brevard County chapter of the NAACP in 1934. He established the organization with the help of the Florida State Teachers Association, drawing on teachers as the base of the membership. By 1941, having been let go from his teaching position because of his political responsibilities, he became an unpaid executive secretary for the NAACP. In that role, he began churning out letters, pamphlets, and articles arguing against second-class citizenship, as evidenced by the unequal salaries earned by Black teachers, underfunded segregated schools, and the disenfranchisement of Black voters. In 1943, he added mob violence, lynching, and police brutality to his subjects of interest, and from that point until his death, Moore personally documented the circumstances of as many reports of lynching in Florida as he was able to find. My grandfather wrote to him in 1946 to commiserate about the lynching in Georgia of two Black couples, who had been set upon by a mob of white men and killed for simply being in the wrong place at the wrong time. Though in another state, he wanted Moore to add it to his documentation.

Indeed, citizenship, violence, protection, and education were as closely tied together in the lives of these activist teachers as were the specifics of educational, curricular, or instructional strategies they employed in their classrooms. This history helps explain why my grandfather, Moore, and others started an organization in Florida that worked to mobilize Black teachers to vote as a means of protecting the citizenship rights of all Black people in the state. Begun in 1944 and named the Progressive Voters League, the organization had five founding members from across the state. Aside from Moore, who served as executive secretary, and my grandfather, who was the league's president, the members included Viola Hill and Reverend E. J. Jackson, who were co–vice presidents, and Emma A. Pickett as the recording secretary. All were also office holders in the NAACP and the Florida State Teachers Association. The membership overlap can be explained by the fact that all three groups were, as was stated in a May 1947 newspaper article, working toward the same goal: "a full program of civil rights for Negro citizens." At a January 1947 meeting of the Black Florida State Teachers Association, during the period when my grandfather served as president, Moore presented an address on behalf of the Progressive Voters League clarifying the intent of the organization relative to education, democracy, and citizenship. "The most important weapon in the struggle for functional democracy is the ballot," he said. "Teachers in the state can help as an organization instead of as individuals. Every teacher in the state should be a registered voter."

The Progressive Voters League began its work by vowing to get rid of the white primary, which it viewed as an impediment to Black political power. These were elections held in some southern states, including Florida, in which only white voters were permitted to participate. White primaries were established in the post-Reconstruction era by state-level Democratic Party officials, first in South Carolina in 1896, followed by Georgia in 1900, Florida, Mississippi, and Alabama in 1902, Texas in 1905, and both Louisiana and Arkansas in 1906. Because winning the Democratic primary in the South almost always meant winning the general election, and because many counties had more Black people in them than white, maintaining their grip on power meant white politicians had a vested interest in disenfranchising Black people. In 1944, working with the NAACP and the Florida State

Teachers Association, Thurgood Marshall argued and won a major case
in which the Supreme Court ruled that the "white only" Democratic
Party primaries were unconstitutional. In the next few years, with the
path to voting for Black people cleared, the Progressive Voters League
got to work, registering over one hundred thousand Black voters in
the Florida Democratic Party. They rallied and organized teachers
throughout the state in conferences, churches, and school auditori-
ums. They wrote letters to local newspapers to introduce readers to
the organization, advocating for political unity and leadership in the
state. In these letters, they challenged "better thinking Negroes" to act
and "not sit around and wait until some selfish, dishonest Negro has
grabbed the political leadership" in your communities. Moore often
signed his letters outlining the group's agenda with "Yours for Democracy in Florida."

One of the organization's major goals was to evaluate and endorse
candidates aligned with their goals and the interests of Black people.
In the 1948 election for the governor of Florida, the League endorsed
Fuller Warren, who won his election by less than twenty-two thousand
votes. In the end, it was the twenty-five thousand Black voters organized by the Progressive Voters League who swung the election his
way. This early success was just the beginning. The votes that the group
provided helped a candidate named William G. Akridge win his 1948
election for state legislative office in Florida's Brevard County. In the
run-up to the election, the group had mailed questionnaires to both
candidates asking about their plans for supporting Black people. The
challenger responded quickly to the mailing, sending his questionnaire
back claiming he would "represent all of the citizens of the county without regard to race, color or creed." The incumbent, however, did not
reply until a few hours before the election and merely responded that
potential voters should judge him by his record. Black people did as he
suggested and voted against him, providing the margin that enabled
Akridge to win. In recognition, after the election Akridge introduced

an anti–mob and lynching bill, which called for the death penalty for
members of mobs who killed their victims. Akridge also introduced a
bill requiring every county to pay teachers equal salaries, solely based
on training and experience, not based on race. These were laws heavily favored by Black teachers, and Black people more generally. The
Progressive Voters League appeared to be well on its way to becoming a political force and began to discuss plans, in collaboration with
the Florida State Teachers Association, to buy land in the state capital
of Tallahassee and build a headquarters from which the two groups
would continue to lobby state officials and organize for Black political
power. Buoyed by these legal breakthroughs and political possibilities,
Moore gathered the courage and political capital to face down another
kind of legal case. It would cost him his life.

In July 1949, four young Black men—Ernest Thomas, Charles
Greenlee, Samuel Shepherd, and Walter Irvin—were accused of rap-
ing a white woman in a case that became known as the Groveland rape
case. A few days after their arrest, one of the accused, Ernest, escaped
from custody. The sheriff raised a thousand-person-strong posse to
recapture him. When they found him, they shot Ernest over four hundred times as he slept under a tree. Police beat Charles, Samuel, and
Walter to coerce confessions. Charles and Samuel did confess. Walter
maintained his innocence. No matter, an all-white jury convicted all
three at trial. Charles was sentenced to life in prison because he was
only sixteen when the alleged rape took place. The other two, Charles
and Samuel, were sentenced to death. At that point, Moore threw
himself into the case, enlisting the help of Thurgood Marshall, the
young activist lawyer he had worked with before on pay equity cases
for Black teachers. Already known to Black people, the Groveland
case thrust Marshall into the national spotlight. After he was shown
evidence proving that the defendants had been brutally beaten before
confessing, Moore publicly called for the prosecution of Sheriff Wil-
lis McCall. The Groveland defendants were convicted in 1949, but in

April 1951, Marshall's efforts led to the convictions being overturned
by the U.S. Supreme Court. As soon as the news reached Florida, pros-
ecutors were prepared to try the young men again.

On November 6, 1951, while Sheriff McCall was driving the two
men back to Lake County for a pretrial hearing, he shot them, killing Shepherd and critically wounding Irvin. The sheriff said the hand-
cuffed prisoners had attacked him and tried to escape. Irvin claimed
that McCall had simply yanked them out of his car and started firing.
The shooting created a national scandal, and Moore began calling
for McCall's indictment for murder. Only six weeks later, on Christmas Day 1951, Moore himself was murdered when a bomb exploded
beneath the floor joists directly under the bed in which he and his wife,
Harriette, slept. He died on the way to the hospital; Harriette died
nine days later. They ended their lives as martyrs, but before that, they
were master teachers in the comprehensive sense of the word, teaching
students to understand, organize against, and find strategies to fight
white supremacy.

The rush to dismantle Black schools and fire impactful Black teachers, like Harry, Harriette, and my grandparents, throughout the previous decade may have been on Dr. Martin Luther King's mind when he
warned, in a 1967 address to Black educators in Georgia, that integration "doesn't mean the liquidation of everything started and developed
by Negroes." To Dr. King, integration went hand in hand with democracy and should be approached with an eye toward achieving "shared
power." He believed that "there are too many Americans, whites and
Negroes, who think of integration merely in aesthetic and romantic
terms, where you just add a little color to a still predominantly white-
controlled power structure." But, he asserted, "I am not one that will
integrate myself out of power." To him, this "shared power" meant that
it should be just as acceptable for a formerly all-white school to have
a Black nurse, teacher, or principal as it was for white administrators
to be at the helm of a newly desegregated Black school welcoming its

first white students. In his vision, integration would be about sharing authority and influence, not dismantling the institutions Black people had built and used to fight for rights and safety.

King understood that schools were a base for Black power and protection. In addition to talking about his fears about the political consequences of the South's implementation of *Brown v. Board of Education* and discarding of Black schools, Dr. King also expressed concern about educational outcomes and warned about Black survival, telling his audience, "I think you are on sound ground in saying that this integration process must not mean Negro annihilation." Ultimately, we know Dr. King's warnings were not heeded. The idea that integration could educate Black and white students equally or promise unfettered and equal access to a high-quality education for Black children would be all too brief. What happened instead was that Black teachers were fired, Black schools were closed, and the burden of integration fell disproportionately on Black students, who were largely left to navigate hostile white environments on their own. At least some Black teachers who had been employed when Brown was decided had different ideas about how the process could have been rolled out.

Following the *Brown* decision, Black teachers, having no reason to believe they would be accepted at white schools and sure Black children would not be loved there, imagined an integration strategy where adults, not children, would be the first to walk through segregated schoolhouse doors. That is the main message of a 1983 oral history interview with Celestine Porter, a Black teacher in North Carolina, who pointed out that:

> Once you grant the idea that a child needs someone to take an interest in them, then that means integration should've been pursued very differently. If they were going to send Black children into the White schools, they should've had some Black teachers there . . . the first people that should've been integrated should

have been teachers and administrations first, but they didn't do that; they moved the children. And most of the students that they moved from the Black schools into the White situation, we as teachers were not there to nurture them, to help them along, to recognize their difficulties, to work with them. When they moved into the White situation, they didn't know the teachers; the teachers were afraid of them.

It remains true that, if you're Black, having a Black teacher makes a difference. It raises the test scores of Black students, changes the way Black students behave in classrooms, and dramatically decreases the chances that a student will ever be suspended. In February 2021, a group of social scientists went over the records of one hundred thousand Black students in North Carolina over a five-year period and found that having even one Black teacher between the third and fifth grade reduced the chance of a Black child dropping out of high school by 39 percent.

Once integrated schools became the law of the land, with many Black teachers fired and white schools refusing to let Black teachers ply their trade with white children, the reality of the nation's unrealized ideal of equal education devastated the Black teaching profession. In the few instances when Black teachers applied to teach in white southern schools, the results were disappointing. Sometimes officials said they were incompetent. Sometimes they said white parents would simply not accept their teaching white students. In the months following the Supreme Court's edict, for instance, district officials in Topeka hired and assigned a Black male teacher to a half-time position at one of the formerly all-white schools. After having made the decision to ease into the *Brown* decree with this one teacher, the school board asked the principal to call up white parents to see if they objected. They all did, but only a few gave reasons. One parent said, "My child is now 12 years of age and is beginning her menstrual period, and this is not the time

of her life to be put in here with a Black teacher, a male." He was fired
before he had even worked a day, and the Board of Education chair
used the negative responses to refuse to hire any other Black teachers.
Writing to one such teacher about why she no longer had a job, the
principal said, "our board must proceed on the assumption that the
majority of people in Topeka will not want to employ Negro teachers
for White children."

In addition to the direct refusal on the part of specific school districts, like Topeka, to hire Black teachers, the White Citizens' Council, a Mississippi-based white supremacist group with a regional reach,
undertook a letter-writing campaign to PTAs throughout Florida, telling parents to insist teachers not permit interactions between Black
and white students in their classrooms. In December 1959, the Southern School News listed a series of incidents, including the arrest in
Dade County, Florida, of three men who, armed with "dummy rifles"
carved out of wood, read a pamphlet in front of a local school slated
for integration that read in part, "Death to all race mixers! Keep your
schools white by massive armed force—Be a Paul Revere! Rally your
neighbors to arms. Shoot the race-mixing invaders!"

With all this taking place, it didn't take long for Black teachers
like my grandparents, the students they taught, and the communities in which they lived to understand that shared power had never
really been on the agenda. Once the celebrations that accompanied the
death of enforced racial segregation ended, it soon became clear that
no one expected white students to come to Black neighborhoods, sit
in classrooms with Black children, or learn from Black teachers. While
the *Brown* decision was to have struck a blow against the inferiority
of Black educational opportunities, for too many white people with
power, Black teachers became a problem they were committed to solving, even though no part of the *Brown* decision ever identified them
as lacking in any way. Most Black parents did not want Black teachers
removed from their children's lives, but once the river started to flow

in that direction, there was no way to turn the tide. Like a collectively experienced night terror from which many awakened screaming, Black people watched as white people in Florida and throughout the South used the *Brown* decision to find ways to weaken the political foundations of Black life by targeting both teachers and Black political organizations that fought for them. The backlash began with an attack on the political organization white Floridians saw as the actual source of the problem: the NAACP.

The Klan had for decades enjoyed healthy support in many parts of Florida, but following news of the *Brown* ruling, crowds swelled at their rallies, as they and other white supremacist groups joined forces to attack both the *Brown* decision and the NAACP with renewed gusto. Politicians also joined the fray, and members of the Florida State legislature announced their intention to run the NAACP out of the state. In 1956, elected officials formed a committee called the Florida Legislative Investigation Committee (FLIC) to study what they termed the subversive activities of the NAACP. State legislatures in Texas, Alabama, Mississippi, Louisiana, Virginia, and North Carolina also ramped up attacks aimed at crippling the reach and impact of the group. In Alabama, state officials ordered the NAACP to stop all business and operations under threat of arrest and imprisonment for any members of the organization who continued their activities. Just as the NAACP was being called on to lend financial, legal, and administrative support to communities facing challenges in implementing the *Brown* decision, chapters of the organization had to fend off high-level and well-organized political attacks against the NAACP itself. Florida went further than most states in its persecution.

From 1956 through 1965, under the guise of investigating communist "subversion," the members of the FLIC committee gave themselves the power to enter residences without warrants, hire informants whose identities were kept secret, obtain and read any requested medical records, and impose penalties without first having to bring charges against an accused. In short, the committee declared war on the NAACP and ignored the Constitution to do it. Headed by a state senator named Charley Johns, the FLIC was commonly referred to as the Johns Committee. Though they did not explain the connection, the elected officials branded those behind efforts to integrate schools as communists and named integration as a first step toward destroying the American family. One of the first people targeted by the committee was a man named Virgil Hawkins. Years before, in April 1949, Hawkins, who had once taught at Bethune-Cookman University, applied for admission to the University of Florida's law school. Despite his academic readiness, because the school was racially segregated, he was not allowed to attend. He had been engaged in a long-running lawsuit to desegregate the institution when he caught the attention of the committee. The FLIC committee counsel, Mark Hawes, grilled Hawkins at a February 1957 hearing, asking if the NAACP was paying his attorney fees. It was not. His attorney was paid for by the Florida State Teachers Association, the Black teacher organization that my grandfather was part of. At the time, understanding the harm that might befall their members and the group if this information came to light, the Black teacher organization listed the financial support they collected to pay the attorney simply as "Project X" in its budget.

The FLIC also aggressively questioned a man named William Fordham, who at the time was the former president of the state level leadership of the NAACP in Florida. The state officials wanted Fordham to tell them about a memo written by the national NAACP office offering advice to local branches on strategies to press for desegregation within their school districts. The FLIC questioning focused specifically on a section of the document advising local branches on how to consult with the national office when potential school desegregation cases were identified, to avoid "compromising" a possible test case. The legislative committee treated the document as a smoking gun, saying it confirmed the NAACP hoped to systematically force white people to accept "full integration" rather than reaching a "compromise" between community members and local school boards. The committee also pressed Reverend A. Joseph Reddick, a minister and administrator for the Miami area branch of the NAACP, after he tried to enroll his daughter in a white school. The FLIC insisted on knowing whether he had received a "national directive" to participate in integration lawsuits. Reddick replied that "the only directive we had was that the Supreme Court has passed a decision and that was the law of the land."

In addition to coming under attack from the legislative committee, both NAACP members and Black children became targets of increasingly threatening behavior. Ruby Hurley, secretary for the southeastern office of the NAACP, wrote the national office in November 1957 to say that white supremacists "threatened to bomb the church and planted colored dolls with cut necks painted with nail polish on the church steps before the meeting to which I spoke on Sunday in Jacksonville."

Despite the FLIC's oppressive tactics and open hostility to the ruling, Black people in Pinellas County, where my grandparents lived, welcomed the ruling and leveraged *Brown* to assist their efforts toward protecting education for Black people. A reverend named Enoch Davis hailed the ruling, saying overturning *Brown* was necessary to restore public faith in the federal government and the rule of law. James Bond, a county official whose job it was to supervise "Negro" education, declared that he thought the decision would dismantle the caste system pervading race relations in Florida. But as was the case elsewhere in the South, the lack of consequences for nonenforcement of *Brown* enabled segregationist political leaders and parents in Florida to continue to ignore the Supreme Court mandate—at the behest of or in conjunction with white parents. In August 1955, a year after the ruling became law, Pinellas County school officials polled members of the white community about their attitudes toward desegregation and found that many supported Massive Resistance. The White Citizens Council of Pinellas presented the school board with letters from white parents who called for continued segregation, and in response, a local politician promised to establish a private tutoring system for students who did not want to attend integrated schools.

The fight for integrated schools extended beyond secondary education. The September following the ruling, the NAACP tested the waters by attempting to help two Black co-valedictorians from St. Petersburg, Florida's all-Black Gibbs High School enroll in St. Petersburg Junior College, a postsecondary institution run by the school board. The college wouldn't admit them. The junior college's principal, John Rembert, publicly commended the school administrators who turned the young men away, saying they took "a sane, unhysterical approach" by not admitting the Black students. According to the historian James Schur, the Pinellas County School Board during this time conducted a survey of white and Black high school seniors to gauge attitudes toward desegregating higher education. The results showed that nearly two-thirds of Pinellas County's white high school seniors believed the state should use all legal means to deny Black people admission to state universities. Unsurprisingly, over 90 percent of Black people surveyed said the state should let them attend schools funded with state money. Listening to the wishes of white people, the Pinellas County School Board rejected a plan by a University of Florida political scientist for limited and gradual integration. Instead, Florida's governor LeRoy Collins and attorney general Richard Ervin created a committee of judges with the sole purpose of offering the state the legal means to ignore *Brown*. One of their first pieces of legislation was called the School Assignment Law, which let districts perpetuate segregation by allowing committee members to assign children to schools based on their judgments about things like aptitude and scholastic proficiency. Though supposedly a race-neutral solution, white and Black children were only ever assigned to schools with members of their own race.

Floyd T. Christian, the superintendent of the Pinellas school district, believed the courts might at least permit postsecondary schools to remain segregated if it promised to deliver on the expired promises of *Plessy v. Ferguson.* In a last-ditch effort to keep from having to admit Black students into white schools, he committed to upgrading facilities in Black neighborhoods, offering new, modern, clean schools that were separate but equal—despite this being precisely the language that had recently been overturned in the *Brown* ruling. Realizing that organizations such as the NAACP and National Urban League could scuttle the plan by merely showing proof that the school board knowingly operated overcrowded and substandard schools for Black people, district officials decided to operate in good faith. Instead of either desegregating or integrating, the school board constructed Gibbs Junior College and eleven other new segregated Black junior or community colleges between 1954 and 1963. By September 1956, Superintendent Christian boasted that such improvements made schools "separate but really equal." Finally, the state was providing schools that matched the resources white schools already enjoyed. But it was a case of too little, too late. Integration was already the law of the land.

In *The Magnificent Twelve,* a book about this crop of new schools written by Dr. Walter Smith, who went on to become a president of Florida A&M, Dr. Smith notes that the institutions were not universally embraced, because Black people saw through and resented white politicians' efforts to keep Black children out of white schools. Some thought Black people should refuse to attend the new junior or community colleges in protest of the continued segregation. The last job my grandfather ever had was at one of these junior colleges. The school, Gibbs Junior College, was named after Jonathan Clarkson Gibbs, a Black Presbyterian minister who served as secretary of state and superintendent of public instruction of Florida from 1868 to 1872. During Reconstruction, he was among the most powerful Black officeholders in the state. When it opened in 1957, the school named after him was the first Black junior college in Florida, and the school's first president was a Black man named John W. Rembert who said his goal was to build a school with a faculty and curriculum that could equip Black students to matriculate and thrive at any four-year college or university in the United States. But at the time, my grandfather and other Black people who worked at the school were seen by some as bowing to racism and segregation. Despite his having served in leadership roles in the organization, my grandfather found himself pitted against NAACP leadership. Yet he was guided by what W. E. B. Du Bois said about Black children's education in 1935: "Theoretically the Negro needs neither segregated schools nor mixed schools. What he needs is education." This is the spirit in which my grandfather embraced a segregated school for Black children.

Despite the competing opinions, according to a 1993 *Tampa Bay Times* article, Gibbs became one of the most popular and respected of the twelve junior colleges. The school started in 1957 with fewer than three hundred students and, given the slow pace of desegregating white schools in the county, grew to 952 students by 1965. The *Times* article features students who attended the school during the ten years it was open and mentions that Eleanor Roosevelt, as well as the late Brooklyn Dodgers president and general manager Branch Rickey, who integrated baseball by hiring Jackie Robinson, once spoke at Gibbs. The students all talked about how impactful the teachers there had been on their future lives. One former student, Eddie Jackson, told the reporter about an administrator at Gibbs named Paul Mohr, who was the college's director of public relations. One day Mohr drove to his home and announced to a surprised Jackson that he was going to be the new editor of the school newspaper. Mohr had just seen a paper Jackson had written for an English class and knew the job would be a good fit for him. When the newspaper won first place as the best junior college newspaper in the Southeast, Mohr gave Jackson a suit to wear to the award ceremony. "We just had the most extraordinary faculty members," Jackson declared. Out of fifty-eight faculty members at Gibbs, fifty-two had master's degrees and three held doctorates. Only ten of the faculty members were white. Of the twelve "Black only" junior colleges started by the state, it was the only one accredited by the Southern Association of Colleges and Schools, and its alumni include medical doctors, lawyers, college professors and administrators, public school teachers, diplomats, science researchers, businesspeople, ministers, and professional athletes.

Another graduate, Virginia Jones Scott, became emotional as she spoke about the influence faculty members at Gibbs had on her life. "Effie Teal taught me really what it meant to work with young people and to love training them. Milton Rooks did also," she said, naming my grandfather. "And Wilma Holloway taught me not to fear numbers. She was my mathematics teacher." Scott credited them with making her feel confident in her abilities and preparing her to thrive when she went on to a white college after completing her course of study at Gibbs. But though successful, embracing a separate but equal school system was no longer either legal, or in vogue. My grandfather spent ten years, among the last of his life, teaching the Black students he so loved at a school that had technically been outlawed and was no longer favored by the Black political establishment. He died a few years before Florida finally opened all schools to Black children in 1971.

Before finally making it possible for Black children to attend any school in the state, token integration came to Pinellas County in the summer of 1961, when two Black students enrolled at St. Petersburg Junior College, one Black student enrolled at Tomlinson Vocational School, and one white student matriculated in a vocational course at otherwise Black Gibbs, where my grandfather taught. No real attempts were made to desegregate elementary-age children until September 1962, when three were allowed by the School Assignment Committee established by the district to help enroll Black students in white schools. A year later, the committee assigned 118 Black children living in white attendance zones to enroll in nearby white schools. While Christian, the superintendent, praised the School Assignment Committee's gradualist approach, the state's NAACP leadership hoped to hasten the process by urging Black people to "shed their shackles of inequality" and demand a plan that required white children to share the burden of integration.

The legal attack on Pinellas County's segregated system began with a class-action suit filed in the U.S. District Court in Tampa on May 7, 1964. Leon W. Bradley Sr., a police officer and vice president of the Clearwater NAACP, met with residents from Clearwater and St. Petersburg, and the group agreed to challenge the school board's gradualist strategy. The NAACP Legal Defense Fund assigned a young attorney named James Sanderlin to the case. In *Bradley v. Board of Public Instruction of Pinellas County,* the lawyer argued that, in defiance of *Brown* and the Civil Rights Act passed that year, less than 2 percent of the county's Black pupils attended desegregated schools, and the district continued to allow white children whose schools appeared poised to desegregate to transfer to all-white schools. Mr. Sanderlin wanted to know why, given this violation, Pinellas County continued to secure federal funds. Perhaps inspired by this line of thinking, a year later, in October 1965, Martin Luther King Jr. tried and failed to convince the Department of Health, Education, and Welfare to deny Chicago Public Schools $30 million in federal funds to penalize the city for its segregated school system. The agency initially withdrew funding, but after an emergency meeting with Richard Daley, the mayor of Chicago, President Lyndon Johnson pressured the Department of Health, Education, and Welfare to restore the funds, and in fact ordered that the employee who had attempted to withhold the money in the first place be fired. For Pinellas County, the threat of a similar lawsuit was enough to force change.

On January 15, 1965, the court ordered the Pinellas County school district to present a plan to eliminate segregation and reassign pupils, faculty, and other personnel on a "non-racial basis." James Sanderlin filed new motions asking the court to increase the speed of their efforts to desegregate schools at the primary and secondary levels. He also charged the district with refusing to recruit teachers from Black colleges, maintaining segregated athletic programs, and allowing white students residing in Black school zones to opt to attend white schools. In March 1969, Judge Joseph Patrick Lieb ordered the district to enact a comprehensive desegregation plan. The first version he approved decreed all schools in the county should have less than 80 percent white enrollment. James Sanderlin, undeterred, petitioned the Fifth Circuit Court of Appeals, which modified the *Bradley* decision on July 29, 1970. They found that during the 1969–70 term, 66 percent of Black people in Pinellas County attended predominantly Black schools. The plan approved by Judge Lieb would have reduced this figure by only 2 percent. In its order, the Fifth Circuit Court demanded all schools be immediately desegregated. White residents of the county disagreed with this order and asked Pinellas Circuit Court judge Charles R. Holley to invalidate it. He did not intervene.

When the Pinellas County School Board finally adopted an effective countywide desegregation program on June 2, 1971, another U.S. Supreme Court decision played a pivotal role. In *Swann v. Charlotte-Mecklenburg*, the justices granted lower courts broad powers to order cross-district busing if patterns of school construction, school abandonment, and pupil assignment indicated that dual systems existed. Sanderlin had filed a motion in May 1971 that urged the district court to use busing to desegregate all schools by September, the beginning of the 1971–72 academic year. Once the Supreme Court delineated the conditions under which busing could be ordered, James Sanderlin's motion was affirmed. This is how Pinellas County became the first school system in Florida to approve an all-inclusive plan to desegregate its schools.

Immediately after the judge overseeing the case ordered full implementation of the new plan in July 1971, white opposition to busing intensified. The United Residents of Pinellas (URP) and Parents

Against Forced Busing (PAFB) joined to oppose court-ordered bus-ing and to argue for the restoration of neighborhood schools. PAFB advocated outright defiance and prepared lawsuits against the board members who had approved the plan, distributed school officials' home telephone numbers, and called for parents to seek exemptions to the compulsory attendance laws by claiming poverty and hardship. When Superintendent Nicholas Mangin invalidated most of the peti-tions, PAFB leaders promised that over twenty thousand pupils would boycott the opening day of school. Ultimately, district records counted only two thousand no-shows, while during the first ten days of the term, almost 4,200 new students matriculated in the system. A few years later, in 1974, I was one of them.

I had not ever thought of myself as a desegregator, whom I envi-sioned as those Black children from documentaries I had watched in school who required troops and police to keep them safe. Yet one day, my husband found my photograph from the fifth grade in 1974. There I was, the only Black, or even Brown, child in a room with twenty-five white students. As I looked at the photograph, I remembered that I was among the first group of Black students bused about forty minutes from our all-Black neighborhood in Clearwater, called "The Heights," to attend school with white children. I could feel the "see your breath" cold winter mornings while I waited for the bus in front of an auto repair shop; the absolute fear of missing the bus back home after school, since it left before any of the others and didn't wait for anyone; and the absence of any memories of birthday parties or after-noons spent chatting with white friends. I didn't have many friends of the kind whom one might see outside school. I remember learning to square dance and to recite from memory all fifty-two prepositions. Other than that, I have nothing particularly traumatizing or momen-tous to report about the experience. I was perfectly tolerated. Perhaps the most notable thing about my integration experience is that, though it took place almost twenty years after *Brown v. Board of Education* decreed that integrated schools were the law of the land, I was still the lone Black student in my school photograph.

When the *Brown v. Board* decision was announced in 1954, my grandparents were still both teaching and administrating at Williams Elementary, the segregated Black school near their home in Clearwater. But by the time I, along with thirty other Black children, matriculated at the newly desegregated Skycrest Elementary in 1974, only my grandmother was still alive to see it. My grandfather died in 1968 never having witnessed his hometown's first steps toward integration. One day, one of the white kids I talked with sometimes, a young white boy, decided to ride the bus home with me. He said he wanted to see my house. I didn't think much of it, and he got onto the bus with me after school with all the other Black students who said nothing to him or me as we rode. If the bus driver found our pairing odd, he kept it to himself. When we arrived at our house, my grandmother was outside watering the garden and, as a southern woman raised to grace, struggled to keep the shock off her face as she offered us water or iced tea. She asked the young man for his mother's phone number so she could let his parents know where he was. He walked around the house for a little bit, looking at every room and constantly saying, "This is nice. This is really nice." I'm pretty sure this was probably the first Black home he had ever entered. We'd had white people over from time to time, though not often and never for very long. His mother came to get him pretty quickly, and she too was nothing but pleasant. She rang the bell and thanked us for looking after her child, whom the whole family had been worried about.

My grandmother and I laughed and laughed after they left, wandering back through the rooms he had walked through repeating, "This is nice." I remember my grandmother saying to me, "Well, sah, Noli, I didn't expect that at all." She also told me to refrain from bringing any more white children home with me without permission. I never did, and that young man never spoke to me again after that visit. That was the extent to which my integration experiences led to any increased cultural acceptance and tolerance. Maybe it had meant something different for my white classmate. I will probably never know. Though my desegregation experience was uneventful, it was blessedly so, given the experiences of children who had decades before tried to integrate schools.

My grandparents were the only members of their tight-knit cohort of teacher-activists, including Harry and Harriette Moore and Noah and Terressa Griffin, who lived long enough to feel the full weight of what the *Brown* decision would mean for Black teachers and students. Once, white supremacists burned a four-foot-tall cross on their front lawn. My grandfather told my mother, his daughter-in law, that the cross burning was a warning urging Black people to stop organizing for civil rights protections. He had worked his whole adult life for equality and equal citizenship and to end the lack of opportunity for Black children under segregation, but he confided in my mother that he had a "powerful fear" that white people wouldn't "love our children over there," meaning in white schools. During the height of his organizing activities, my grandfather hired a driver to accompany him as he drove through the rural, dark, lonely Florida countryside. The driver carried a gun, which my father said was likely why my grandfather died from natural causes rather than facing a violent end. Years after he had passed, my mother shared that he died mourning and feared forever lost the pre-*Brown* Black educational ecosystem: schools with Black teachers who loved Black students and would teach them how to survive, all while fighting for their lives and futures outside the classroom.

My grandmother never told me so directly, but as I learned to hear the emotion underneath the words and fill in the silences when she shared stories about her and my grandfather, about their students, and who and how they wanted them to grow to be in the world, I realized she, too, was mourning. She realized that most Black kids would never regain what had been dismantled. I conjured the rubble of the school around the corner. That school and all that the Black community built there was a certain kind of dream white administrators killed, ostensibly in the name of Black progress. Remnants of ruin were all that remained. My grandmother was fired from her position at Williams Elementary in 1966. A few years later, with her husband gone, she decided she would try to substitute teach in white schools from time to time to fill her days. She loved teaching and thought she might be a stable and supportive presence in the lives of the Black students who were in desegregated schools but who she had started to hear were housed in classrooms together, cordoned off from most of the white students in the school and struggling academically. She thought she could help. But the substitute-teaching assignments she was given were to teach white children in "hard to manage" classrooms. They wouldn't listen to her. They laughed and taunted her. She subsequently gave up on substitute teaching. The last time my grandmother taught a class was in a desegregated school inside which white and Black children remained separated and where she was not allowed to teach the Black students whom white teachers had given up on. In our current moment, we are left to wonder what might have happened to Black children if Black teachers like Mrs. Davenport, Harry and Harriette Moore, Noah and Terressa Griffin, and Milton and Evelyn Rooks Sr. had desegregated the teaching staffs in white schools ahead of the students. We will ultimately never know, but I believe my father exemplifies why even asking the question matters.

If in a Black community and in Black schools my father had thrived, as one of the first to integrate a white institution, his demons, as his mother described his drinking, took over his life. I asked him once if he regretted not becoming a lawyer and stepping into the civil rights fray as his parents had wanted. His answer was clear. He did not regret it at all. He had long since stopped believing the law alone could heal the hate he grew to know so well. He didn't know what else was required, but the aftermath of the *Brown* decision taught him that achieving Black educational access would require more than the endorsement of the Supreme Court of the United States. He no longer even really believed that integration was a cure. For my father, the ruling was just a piece of paper that would not protect or make safe the Black children being blown into white classrooms by the winds of change. My grandparents thought of themselves as preparing my father to be the Thurgood Marshall of his generation. They believed he would attend law school, graduate, open a practice in Florida, and fight for Black rights in the state and the nation. They didn't believe, despite any progress they or their friends had made in trying to secure Black rights, that white supremacy in the state was near to ending, nor did they think Black equality was right around any type of corner they could see. Struck by Marshall's example of principled resistance to white supremacy, they thought of the law as the magic bullet that could keep them and theirs safe. They didn't know that the *Brown* decision, one of the surest examples of the power of the law to protect Black citizenship, would signal the beginning of the end of the community they saw, knew, and had prepared Black children to survive within. They did not foresee having to refight battles supposedly long won over the humanity and intelligence of children in my father's or subsequent generations.

4

"WE, TOO, HAD GREAT EXPECTATIONS. AND THEN WE WENT TO SCHOOL."

Though I never asked my father, Milton Rooks Jr., much about how he was as a child, I imagine his first lesson in what he could expect from life as a southern Black boy came when he was quite small. He grew up in Clearwater, Florida, in a single story, three-bedroom, one-bathroom house with a small front yard. The road out front was packed earth that remained unpaved until I was almost eight, and the house was surrounded by others that Black people had built for themselves, stitching together a community that would come to be known as the Heights. My father had been born in the house next door, in what folks in New Orleans would call a "shotgun shack." His cousins, uncles, and other kin, blood or not, all lived nearby. His parents taught in the local school, and he was raised to succeed in the complicated ecosystem of a Black community, which served as a buffer against the hostility at its edges. Only much, much later would anyone think Milton might be able to take a place in a white one. Even then, it would be to become like Thurgood Marshall, bringing back tools to fight ideas, policies, and practices that proclaimed Black inferiority. His parents imagined his learning would be applied within a world where most shared his skin tone and the idea of success was always tied to uplifting not just his family but all Black people. It was a heavy burden for him, but his early educational experiences made him confident he could bear it. Then educational desegregation thrust him into a world for which he wasn't built, and the load became much harder to carry.

My father's high school yearbook shows Black marching bands performing, playing, and twirling through the segregated streets of Clearwater—showing off and feeling free. He graduated as class valedictorian, senior class president, captain of the basketball team, editor of the yearbook, and member of the band, in which he played violin. Flipping through the book's pages, I see Black students as prom kings and queens or participating in chess and political science clubs, as well as Black teachers, coaches, custodians, cafeteria workers, and administrative employees—all there to enrich the lives of their students and provide Black children educational love and support. Notes in the yearbook include nicknames, dreams, and lots of excitement about the future. One classmate left my father this message: "We can because we think we can."

The images on those pages reflected the supportive educational environment that his parents had helped foster and that the Supreme Court's decision had effectively wiped out. Black children like my father, who was born in the 1930s, lived most of their educational lives before the passage of the Civil Rights Act or bills that made it safer for them to move through the world (or at least attempted to). Part of what he learned at school, at home, and in his community was how to survive in a country where Black civil and human rights were an unsecured half thought. Still, I have his yearbooks and know that, as he left high school to attend college at Howard University in Washington, D.C., he was full of hope.

Six months after Milton settled into his college dorm, in March 1956, Congressman James C. Davis from Georgia declared the fledgling educational desegregation efforts in the capital both "a scholastic failure" and, as an experiment in human relations, "a nightmare." Across the country, in Inglewood, California, an opinion writer inaccurately informed readers: "In Washington's integrated schools, armed police now patrol the halls to protect white students and teachers from Negro jungle violence. Slashings, knifings, assaults, indecent exposures, and sex incidents are so rampant throughout the district's integrated system that white students are virtually deserting the schools en-masse." Several months later, though journalists and educational officials believed desegregation in the district had proceeded smoothly and without the outbreaks of violence witnessed in the South, Representative Davis chaired a full-scale congressional investigation into what had gone *wrong* with desegregating schools in the nation's capital. The final report, which Representative Davis signed along with two other southern congressmen, declared that integrating schools in the district had "seriously damaged the public school system in the District of Columbia" and that, taken as a whole, the evidence "points to a definite impairment of educational opportunities for members of both white and Negro races as a result of integration, with little prospect of remedy in the future." Only two members of the six-person District of Columbia Committee, also called the Davis Subcommittee—Representatives A. L. Miller of Nebraska and DeWitt S. Hyde of Maryland—disagreed with the southern majority. They said the report drew unsupported conclusions and declared that the final document "does not appear to be well-balanced or objective." Ignoring this dissent, the southern representatives published their findings in the summer of 1956, reprinting thousands of copies and distributing them throughout the South.

As violently sensational battles against integration dragged on in the South and big cities found that there were fewer and fewer white children to participate in desegregation plans, policymakers both in northern cities and at the federal level began to battle integration on an ideological level. By the time my father arrived, Washington, D.C., was poised to star in a character drama about the limits of desegregation, exposing the meager range of strategies adopted to address the undereducation of Black children clustered in majority-Black cities north of the Mason-Dixon Line—the imaginary fence separating the former slaveholding South from its northern neighbors, where racism was not always of an obvious sort.

As but two examples of the national reach and impact of Representative Davis's report, in a television appearance during the 1957 Little Rock crisis—when President Eisenhower dispatched the 101st Airborne to the city to help nine Black teenagers desegregate the local high school—Arkansas's governor, Orval Faubus, urged his audience to request copies of the report, warning that the white children locked out of Little Rock's closed Central High School could lose an entire year of schooling, if need be, and "still be educationally ahead of students in integrated Washington, D.C." In Virginia, Governor J. Lindsay Almond Jr. went on television to rail against educational integration and addressed some of his comments "to those who defend or close their eyes to the livid stench of sadism, sex, immorality, and juvenile pregnancy infesting the mixed schools of the District of Columbia and elsewhere."

As a student at the historically Black Howard University, my father was relatively insulated from this cultural and social backlash to integration. He continued to thrive in a Black educational setting, and in 1960, he left D.C. for law school at the Golden Gate College School of Law in San Francisco. There, for the first time, he had white teachers and experienced the sensation of being one of only a handful of Black students in classrooms filled with white faces. All the professors at the law school were white men who had not had much, if any, experience teaching Black people and, as least as far as my father was concerned, were in the habit of making Black people prove over and over that they deserved to have a seat in their classrooms. When my father spoke, his answers were dismissed as wrong or facile. Some of his classmates soon learned it was to their benefit to take his answers, rephrase them, and offer them to the professors, who rewarded them with warm smiles and nodding heads.

Milton's experience reflected the trauma Black students suffered as they desegregated public schools in states above the Mason-Dixon Line, where displays of racism were often mocking, disdainful, pitying, and sword sharp in their ability to cut the unsuspecting into tiny bits. It destroyed confidence, shook will, sowed doubt, murdered souls— quietly, sure, but still as completely as could a mob of white racists setting their cowardice, rage, and anger loose upon the defenseless.

The attempts to desegregate classrooms in Washington, D.C., immediately after *Brown* were not physically violent as in cities like Boston, where white people hurled bricks at buses carrying Black children, or Mansfield, Texas, where federal marshals patrolled school grounds with guns to stop whites from preventing Black students from even registering in their local high school. Still, some white parents pulled their kids out of public schools and sent them to private school, while student opponents of desegregation organized walkouts after attending school with Black children for a few weeks. When reporters asked white students why they were protesting, one explained, "It might work out if [integration] had started in kindergarten. The trouble is that half of us have been brought up to hate them, and half of us have been brought up to get along with them."

Another student struggled to articulate why he even opposed integrating schools, saying he was fighting desegregation but admitting, "I don't know why, but colored are made to stay by themselves and we by ourselves." Yet another student presented a "petition of grievances" to reporters who asked students why protest was necessary, listing concerns such as "We don't want to shower with them," referring to Black students, and noting that none of the striking students believed that "mob rule is the best way to stop integration but if other actions fail this must be resorted to."

As happened in other major cities in the years following the *Brown* ruling, D.C.'s population of white schoolchildren dropped, with some families leaving the city entirely to move to overwhelmingly white suburbs. Though in the last year of segregation schools in Washington, D.C., were already majority Black, the number of white students continued to decline precipitously, and by 1959 74.1 percent of students enrolled in the school system were Black. Initially, the political and educational focus on schools was not about race and access to schools but rather about the rising alarm by white district officials over how the low level of academic achievement among Black students was dragging down the whole system. When the results of the first district-wide achievement tests were published in 1955, they showed the district had tested sixty-four thousand Black and forty-one thousand white students and now knew that the typical Black fifth grader in D.C. was working at the national fourth-grade level in math and at the third-grade level in reading. The scores came as a surprise because, previously, Black and white students had always used different sets of tests and not all Black children had been tested, so no one knew there were differences.

As the population of children in the schools became Blacker, school policies changed as well. By the mid-1960s, with the demographic change almost complete, school officials implemented a tracking system that grouped students into categories ranging from "basic" to "honors," resulting in schools beginning to educate students separately and unequally in the same school buildings. The district had a four-track system: a rigorous program for gifted children, a college preparatory track for children who knew college was in their future and who wanted to ensure they took a relevant course of study, a general education program for students not planning to go to college but who would immediately enter the workforce, and a remedial curriculum that helped stragglers catch up on basic literacy and foundational math skills. Almost from the start, Black students came to make up almost all the students on the lowest-performing level. By 1958, Assistant School

Superintendent Francis Gregory, one of the system's top Black officials and himself a graduate of D.C. schools, tried to soothe rising concerns about the different types of education on offer in the same school buildings and defended the racial imbalance by saying:

> No one who goes into a school and sees a slow group made up 80 or 100 per cent of Negro students should feel any resentment. It would be a disservice to group them otherwise. For some time more children in the upper groups will be white and more in the lower groups will be Negro. It takes a while to overcome the results of segregation and cultural disabilities.

In addition to academic challenges, as school desegregation continued to pick up steam, a variety of mutual aid and charitable organizations began to raise an alarm about the unsustainable levels of poverty in the city and reported that D.C. schools received about seven hundred requests a month for clothing and more than six hundred requests a month for shoes just so Black children could attend school. Most of the thefts reported in D.C. schools between 1956 and 1959 involved food. In response, the district started a campaign for public contributions to help schools serve daily lunches for almost seven thousand hungry children in elementary schools.

This is the context into which President Lyndon Johnson introduced his Great Society, or War on Poverty agenda—a series of federal programs that carried the ambitious goal of eliminating poverty as a way of eradicating racial injustice. Johnson, who said he'd been sensitized to the debilitating nature of poverty and racial exclusion after tutoring and teaching Chicano children during the summers when he was a college student, viewed education as a solution for both ills. Instead of equalizing access to well-resourced, high-performing schools, Johnson embraced a strategy focused on saving preschool-age children. In the process, he shifted the public policy conversation from one centering race to one focused on poverty. To operationalize the effort, President Johnson authorized the funding and nationalization of Head Start, a program he said would prepare underprivileged children for kindergarten, give them access to medical and dental treatment, and also provide counseling to parents to support them in "improving the home environment."

At a ceremony in the White House Rose Garden in May 1965, he claimed the program meant that "nearly half the preschool children of poverty will get a head start on their future" and touted it as an attempt to disrupt the multigenerational cycle of poverty for "disadvantaged" preschool children. "I believe that this is one of the most constructive, and one of the most sensible, and also one of the most exciting programs that this nation has ever undertaken." The president warned that though he thought the federal government had a role to play in ensuring equal access to educational opportunity, he didn't think mere legislation, no matter how bold, could do the job alone if Black people did not fix their family structures and work harder to cure the pathology within their homes. This language owed a debt to a social scientist and senator named Daniel Patrick Moynihan, who had released an influential government report in 1965: "The Negro Family: The Case for National Action." In it, Moynihan claimed that the social dysfunction and cultural chaos bubbling up in majority-Black urban communities and the rise in single-parent households were at the heart of what he termed a "tangle of pathology" defining Black culture. Black people in the United States, Moynihan argued, suffered under the bitter, emasculating legacy of slavery, and in response had adapted to a matriarchal family structure that was seriously out of line with the rest of American society, malforming communities and damaging Black children.

The year before Moynihan's report, another social scientist, James Coleman, a Johns Hopkins sociologist, was charged with fulfilling one of the requirements of the Civil Rights Act of 1964: investigating "the lack of availability of equal educational opportunities for individuals by reason of race, color, religion, or national origin in public educational institutions." Though the scope of the report was meant to be financial, looking at funding and resource distribution among the country's schools, Coleman broadened his purview to include the impact of teachers, family members, and neighborhoods in helping children learn. In what was at the time one of the largest social science surveys ever conducted, Coleman concluded that money had little to do with Black children's academic achievement. Though the 737-page report, published in July 1966, acknowledged that separate and unequal schools continued to exist more than a decade after *Brown* and found that, nationally, Black students were regularly testing several grade levels below their white counterparts in math and reading—a difference he termed an "achievement gap"—Coleman claimed that neither the condition of a school nor the funding it received was the most important factor in a child's educational success. Instead, he said—in apparent agreement with President Johnson's assessment—a student's family background, combined with a diverse socioeconomic mix in classrooms, was the biggest determinant of how well a Black child would learn.

One of Coleman's major findings was that, unlike white students, Black children felt that their future was not under their control. When those who participated in one of the surveys included in Coleman's study were asked, "What's more important in school, good luck or hard work?" Black children said, "Good luck, because it's not in my hands." Coleman said such responses showed "that children from advantaged groups assume that the environment will respond if they are able enough to affect it; children from disadvantaged groups do not make this assumption but in many cases assume that nothing they will do can affect the environment—it will give benefits or withhold them but not as a consequence of their own action."

Indeed, this aligns with insight offered by Black Panther leader Huey P. Newton in his 1973 autobiography, *Revolutionary Suicide*.

In it, he challenges the idea of Black family dysfunction and raises the specter of equal educational opportunity as a myth, noting that his experience in Oakland schools had been structured to block the American dream:

> This was how we grew up—in a close family with a proud, strong, protective father and a loving, joyful mother. . . . We shared the dreams of other American children. In our innocence we planned to be doctors, lawyers, pilots, boxers, and builders. How could we know then that we were not going anywhere? Nothing in our experience had shown us yet that the American dream was not for us. We, too, had great expectations. And then we went to school.

When finding that, upon graduation, he and his friends "were ill-equipped to function in society, except at the bottom," Newton speculated that school leaders "knew what they were doing, preparing us for the trash heap of society, where we would have to work long hours for low wages." But rather than viewing these feelings as valid responses to societal inequality, Coleman's report paved the way for others to identify Black people's attitude as the problem. The problem with the report was not in the data compiled but in Coleman's interpretation of the findings.

The well-known and well-understood negative relationship between poverty and educational attainment is part of the reason reactions ranged from consternation to outright disbelief when Coleman dismissed the efficacy of spending money to positively influence Black achievement. In response, a staff member for the Advisory Commission on Intergovernmental Relations, a politically bipartisan commission, said: "We don't mean to write off Coleman," before objecting, "But we also don't want to say that putting more money into schools isn't going to help. Spent wisely, it helps." Coleman's findings were so counterintuitive that the report was debated at congressional hearings, written about in newspapers and magazines, and assigned as required reading to students in colleges and universities. When asked why there was an initial reluctance to accept the report, Coleman later speculated that white families likely took issue with his recommendation for social and economic diversity, explaining that white parents wanted to feel justified in moving to the suburbs and enrolling their children in good, majority-white schools, despite what impact it might have on the schools and students left behind. Coleman's report did not collect data to understand—or even mention—white resistance to Black education and its impact on educational outcomes.

Decades after its release in 1966, scholars came to question, if not flat-out dismiss, Coleman's methods and conclusions. In a retrospective published in 2016, Stanford professor Caroline Hoxby said that "Coleman's analysis was not only wrong but generated misunderstandings that remain sadly pervasive today." That conclusion may have been drawn by more contemporary scholars, but in the mid-1960s, other researchers latched on to Coleman's conclusions about the importance of family background, using this as a launchpad to weave tales about what was lacking in Black communities and resurface eugenicist ideas. Moynihan, for instance, a politician and Harvard professor, who touched on similar themes in his own report published almost two years after Coleman's, strongly cosigned the latter's findings. In speeches and articles, Moynihan offered an enthusiastic embrace of Coleman's conclusion that families mattered more than school funding in terms of educational achievement. In fact, he wrote in an article for the *New York Times* that "The least promising thing we could do in education would be to spend more money on it."

What this all means is that when Milton entered Howard University, social science evidence—specifically the doll study conducted by Drs. Clark, which showed that segregation led to feelings of inadequacy for Black students and an unhealthy embrace of white supremacy in white students—had helped convince the nine justices on the

Supreme Court that segregated, underfunded, and unequal education damaged the psyches of Black and white students alike. But by the time he returned in the spring of 1965, after dropping out of law school and this time with my mother and me along for the ride, the social science evidence then in vogue with politicians, philanthropists, and policy-makers claimed that addressing and correcting systems that produced inferiority or supremacy were a waste of time. New so-called evidence based on government-sponsored research reports had determined that Black people and their family structures, poverty, and culture were the actual problems in need of correcting.

This is the political and scholarly context within which, in August 1965, an educational researcher named Rose Mukerji assembled a team to produce *Roundabout,* an educational television show meant to bol-ster the educational achievement of poor preschool Black children in Washington, D.C. A precursor of *Sesame Street, Roundabout* was based on the new and intriguing idea that television might be a good way to cheaply but productively educate preschool-age Black children who the rising tide of sociological studies and policy briefs said were, even before they entered a kindergarten classroom, already so far behind educationally that they might never catch up. Some scholarship at the time had also begun to show that to avoid feelings of isolation and alienation, Black children needed to see teachers and media images who looked like them.

The show, termed a "national demonstration project" in the August 1966 report Mukerji wrote summarizing the project for federal offi-cials, was designed to provide young viewers with experiences and guided activities to "extend their horizons in the creative arts, music and dance, science, literature and drama, and to deepen their awareness and understanding of interpersonal relations." Shot through with the thinking and conclusions of Moynihan and Coleman, the *Roundabout* experiment rested on the assumption, sometimes stated, sometimes not, that educational impediments for poor Black children lay within the children and their cultures, families, and environments. "Cultural deprivation, poor background; poor homes or broken homes are responsible for some of the deficiencies" among Black students, Mukerji wrote, hoping to collect money from President Johnson's War on Poverty program. "The culturally deprived child is handicapped in learning to read and lacks support within the home to help him overcome his deficiencies."

In addition to providing academic support, *Roundabout* was conceived as a way to acculturate and educate children without the help of families—much as Indigenous children had been removed from their homes in the nineteenth century to unlearn the ways of their parents and communities. The show promoted the idea that its potential viewers didn't have the necessary preparation for school because—though this would seem to be true of most children that age—they didn't know how to listen to or follow instructions, or how to behave in a preschool classroom, presumably as a result of being both Black and poor. In another report published in 1968, Mukerji wrote that *Roundabout* had been designed not only to teach children to read and write but to expose them to the values, norms, and ways of speaking in dominant society.

To program consultants like Kenneth Clark, who understood the issue from a far more nuanced perspective, *Roundabout* as an educational experiment was inadequate and maybe even a step backward. He questioned the emphasis on "the children are to blame" and the "no books in the home" theories about why Black children fell behind. He said he "looked in general for a program which addressed itself directly to the problem of teaching efficiency and the problem of adequate supervision and general accountability for effective education within the schools, but I looked in vain." The show might have been innovative, but to Clark, it was based on flawed social science and lacked attention to basic rules of pedagogy.

An innovative aspect of the project was that these extended horizons were to be imparted by a Black host, though even this decision would be based on racist and flawed logic. Influenced by Moynihan's research, the show's creators decided that the young children they wanted to reach most needed a Black man in their lives, which they assumed the children watching the show did not have at home. They also decided they did not want a trained professional in the role because someone untrained would, they believed, be more recognizable to preschool Black children.

The search for the new host centered on high-poverty areas in Washington, D.C., like the Cardozo neighborhood. Flyers announcing auditions said the show was looking for a "young father type" with the personality and ability to communicate with preschool children who come from "disadvantaged homes." The flyers were circulated in churches, barber shops, and community centers, and the initial casting call drew three hundred Black men. That number was cut to eleven candidates who were asked to make an audition tape, which consisted of a performance with preschool children and one or two live animals. The group was whittled down to three candidates, with my father ultimately winning the role. The producers chose Milton not because of previous skill or expertise, but because he was an attractive and well-spoken Black man who the researchers believed could serve as a teacher, role model, and father figure to the Black children who were meant to make up the show's primary audience. He also later learned that he impressed the non-Black educators, consultants, directors, government officials, and producers by being so "effortlessly articulate."

His name on the show was Mr. Jeffers, Jim Jeffers to be exact. During the initial production meeting, my mother tells me that Milton listened perplexed as the non-Black producers summarized the educational needs of Black children. Having read the concluding report Mukerji submitted to federal officials reviewing the progress she was making on her grant, I can assume what he heard was something about Black children having "a paucity of experiences that can serve as background for school learning, an inadequate conceptual base, limited vocabulary and communication skills, particularly verbal, lack of familiarity with school values, inappropriate attitudes toward school, and depressed self-concepts." This is what Mukerji thought to be true. Though the project was supposed to be helpful for Black children, there was nothing positive about the families, communities, neighborhoods, cultures, or children *Roundabout* was designed to serve discussed in that first meeting, or in the reports and updates submitted.

No matter. In a 1967 article in the *Chicago Defender* covering the series launch, the reporter hailed the show as one of the "most influential productions ever seen on the airwaves." The goal, the article said, was for the show to function similarly to a Head Start class, and the reporter particularly praised Jim Jeffers, my father's character on the show. But it is telling that, unlike the critically acclaimed show that would follow in *Roundabout*'s footsteps, *Sesame Street,* this early experiment focused less on skills like counting or identifying colors, and more on trying to "acquaint" the children with "skills" such as "how hinges work" and how buildings are constructed, in addition to subjects like personal relationships.

Reading through the sample scripts included with the funding reports, I had a bit of a shock when I realized that some of my early memories of my father were wound up in the show. A song he taught me called "Dem Bones," about which bones connected to which other bones in the human body, was from one of the show's segments and based on the idea that teaching children songs was a good way to ensure the lesson was fun, learned, and retained. I can attest: I can still tell you which bones go where by singing parts of the song he taught me when I was around three or four. In another activity, he would pat his thighs rhythmically, singing, "We are going on a bear hunt" and ask me to sing back answers describing what I saw. I would squeal when the pace of our "walking," as represented by his quickened patting, turned to a run, because we had encountered a bear hiding in a cave. At certain points he would say something open-ended, patting and chanting, like "I see a bush, what's growing out of it," and then wait for me to say something like "leaf" or "flower" or "stick." His leg patting would quicken as we "walked" over to the bush and pulled the leaf out before heading to another site on the imagined nature walk. This activity had been used on *Roundabout* to teach children to engage in storytelling and participatory learning.

Given that I remember these lessons half a century after they were taught, I did not find it hard to believe, as producers told their funders, that my father made a significant impact on his young viewers. Sometimes, they said, instead of referring to the program by name, the preschoolers called *Roundabout* "The Jim Jeffers Show" or told teachers when they thought it was "time for Jim Jeffers." Children referred to the show's theme song as "Jim Jeffers's Song" and sometimes claimed expertise by saying, "I know 'cause I saw it on Jim Jeffers."

Because the show was taped in Washington, D.C., sometimes Jim Jeffers would show up at local Head Start centers just to say hello. He was always immediately surrounded by children who sent out the call around the facility, "Hey, Jim Jeffers is here!" As he sat on the rug with them, they talked over each other discussing what they saw on television. Watching the programs in groups in their preschools, the young people told teachers they liked the show because of Jim and felt like, "Hey, he's talking to US!" One little Black girl pouted that she didn't like Mr. Jeffers anymore, because he "didn't wave at her" from the television set. Two little Black boys who were around four argued that he might be able to beat up both Batman and Superman, before deciding that Superman would probably win. Another little Black girl, who was five, declared herself unhappy with him after he promised on the show that they were going to the grocery store to shop, and then, after going shopping on the show, didn't actually show up at her house to pick her up and take her out.

Though *Roundabout* originally aired in the Washington, D.C., area and was aimed at Black children, it was syndicated and made its way to places like Buffalo, Chicago, and rural Kansas. Some white adult viewers explicitly wrote or called the station to express their appreciation for having "Jim" come into their homes through television because, they said, it helped broaden their children's experience in a significant interpersonal way with a person of another race. Though having their children sit in classrooms with Black children to learn might have been too much to ask, white families were enthusiastic about watching a Black person from afar. In addition to shaping familiarity by including a likable Black man, producers also focused quite a bit on shaping the set and home where Jim lived and worked. They wanted the house to look like what they thought they would find in an impoverished urban area. They settled on the look of a row of houses set directly on the sidewalk and with a pair of steps to serve as a gathering place for "Jim" and his friends. A companion set was a basement workshop with ample workspace, electricity and water, tools, and an easy chair.

The show seemed to have developed a solid audience, and Mukerji and her team were pleased that their efforts to relate to their young viewers were working—the underlying assumption being that if the children saw themselves, or children very much like themselves, on television, this would raise their self-esteem. The results of this approach would not be immediately discernible, but the beneficial effects of portraying Black and other non-white children in mass media were becoming abundantly clear given the feedback the show received from viewers, as well as the increasing calls from academics and psychologists alike for just this type of inclusive programming. Mukerji wrote in one of her reports to funders that "More opportunities should be made available through the mass media, particularly television, for men and for members of minority groups to reach the total population of young pre-school children." They were a bit ahead of their time in recognizing the educational importance of having diverse representations available to students in the media, but that basic idea was one that reached a fully flowered state with another show called *Sesame Street.*

Though *Roundabout* would ultimately fail to last beyond that one season that began in September of 1967, two years after it was canceled, a filmmaker named Joan Ganz Cooney named the show as one of her sources of inspiration for a new show "to woo youngsters into an awareness of the alphabet, numbers, healthy social relationships, lessons in logic and thoughtful behavior." Her "target child," too, was the four-year-old, inner-city Black youngster. According to scholar Robert Morrow, who has written a definitive history of *Sesame Street,* Cooney's position on how the program might appeal to a diverse audience of preschoolers was sharpened after she had watched episodes

> of a little-known educational show then on the air. With funding from the United States Office of Education (OE), WETA, the educational station in Washington, D.C., produced *Roundabout* especially for African-American preschoolers. An African-American man, Milton Rooks, was the host of the program, on which he taught some science and math. He also introduced viewers to people children might typically meet in their neighborhoods, such as barbers and policemen. The show included unrehearsed children expressing themselves creatively through music, dance, and puppetry.

Cooney concluded by saying the show was "well produced," despite it not having "won a large 'at-home' audience," as she thought she might do with *Sesame Street.*

Unlike the team who created *Roundabout,* with *Sesame Street* a board of experts from the diverse fields of education, child development, psychology, medicine, the social sciences, the arts, and advertising advised Cooney and her team, which placed a premium on the inclusion of Black perspectives. A January 1970 *Ebony* profile of the show included a photo of Cooney flanked by a team of Black women, including the head of Seattle Head Start and the principal of a New York preschool. Chester Pierce, a Black psychiatrist, is credited with crafting the show's "hidden curriculum" to build up the self-worth of Black children through the presentation of positive Black images. He also insisted the show present an integrated, harmonious community to challenge the marginalization Black children routinely saw on television and elsewhere in society. Indeed, the psychological and educational benefit of Black children seeing and learning from people who looked like them on television was a driver behind the creation, in 1968, of Black Psychiatrists of America, a group put together by Pierce to address the lack of focus on Black people within the profession and to challenge their white colleagues to think of racism in a new way.

Created on April 4, 1968, in the wake of the assassination of Martin Luther King Jr., the Black Psychiatrists of America knew that racism was built into systems and structures, including psychiatry itself. For this reason, as some of them put it in 1973, they pushed the idea that "institutional change (as opposed to personality change) are needed to root out and eliminate racism." Pierce started the organization and took on the role of president because he was extremely concerned about what he considered to be the negative influence of television on the self-concepts of Black children, telling his colleagues in 1970: "Many of you know that for years I have been convinced that our ultimate enemies and deliverers are the education system and the mass media," adding that the organization must, "without theoretical squeamishness over correctness of our expertise, offer what fractions of truth we can to make education and mass media serve rather than to oppress the black people of this country." It was Pierce who first coined the now widely used term "microaggression." It came about as he began thinking about how to describe the impact of the plethora of negative images of Black people in television commercials and programs that he believed collectively represented a subliminal attack on the developing psyches of Black children. The issue was personal to him. He had a three-year-old daughter of his own. As a result, when asked, he eagerly agreed to serve as a senior adviser on *Sesame Street*.

Sesame Street first aired on public television stations across the country in 1969. Much like on *Roundabout,* the adults, children, and puppets lived, worked, and played together on a street in a Black urban neighborhood. Also, similar to *Roundabout,* early episodes of *Sesame Street* featured a Black man as a "role model." This one was named Gordon, and he was a schoolteacher. Gordon was married to Susan, an actress named Loretta Moore Long who was also a doctoral student at UMass Amherst. In her unpublished dissertation, Long wrote that "*Sesame Street* has incorporated a hidden curriculum . . . that seeks to bolster the Black and minority child's self-respect and to portray the multi-ethnic, multi-cultural world into which both the majority and minority child are growing."

At the same time, while secondhand integration was being celebrated, outside the television screen a war against integration was still being waged. The coupling of educational access, opportunity, and achievement to the presence or absence of Black poverty and to proclivities assumed to be innate in Black people, along with increasing calls for Black Power, marked a new chapter in the story of integration as educational policy in the United States. As civil rights activists outside the South began to propose and demand concrete strategies to integrate neighborhoods, schools, and jobs, in the urban North white community members perceived the advances of Black people as taking something away from them, and the more advances Black people made, the louder were the calls for law and order.

For their part, Black young people felt themselves to be under attack, if not at war with the police. Soon, images of Black people fighting back against police, whom they often called racists or, sometimes, pigs became more common. As Black people battered back against the walls of white oppression with calls for power that reached increasingly loud decibels too hard to ignore and uprisings that rocked urban areas like Watts, Newark, and Detroit, the phrase "law and order" became a central part of the political prescription for Black education. White politicians assured listeners that the issue was no longer about Black children needing police protection so they could attend schools with white children. Now, increasingly, newspaper and television images of Black children interacting with police told a story about how Black children needed to be sequestered in schools with each other, and, given the predisposition to inferiority and rampant pathologies that by then had become widely understood to be present in Black communities, it naturally followed that white people were now the ones who needed protection.

Frank Rizzo, who started his career as Philadelphia's police commissioner before becoming mayor in 1972, rose to prominence just as this national "law and order" wave crested and replaced the fading sounds of a once-sung chorus about how "we" shall "overcome." In both roles, Rizzo waged a violent war against Black schoolchildren. One of the first incidents involving Rizzo was centered on an all-white boarding school for orphaned boys located in North Philadelphia, an overwhelmingly Black and poor-to-working-class area of the city. Black people looked at the all-white school, named Girard College, in their all-Black neighborhood and saw it as a symbol of exclusion. Stephen Girard, the nineteenth-century Philadelphia banker and financier after whom the school was named, had stipulated in his last will and testament that the terms of the endowment he left the school included barring Black children from ever stepping foot on the property. When *Brown* outlawed legalized segregation in schools, Girard, which by then was run by the city, found itself in violation of the law. But instead of desegregating, city officials circumvented the *Brown* decision by turning control over to a private board made up of school alumni. This maneuver disturbed the president of Philadelphia's NAACP chapter, Cecil B. Moore, who, in response, organized a variety of community protests aimed at forcing Girard to desegregate. This type of activism brought him into regular confrontation with Frank Rizzo, who at that time was the deputy police commissioner. Moore said Rizzo was upholding segregation by helping schools evade implementation of the *Brown* decision; Rizzo retorted that the police worked to uphold only "law and order," not segregation.

In August 1966, just as *Roundabout* was getting started, Rizzo's boss, the police commissioner Edward J. Bell, left town on vacation for a few weeks and asked Rizzo to serve as commissioner on an interim basis. Rizzo accepted the assignment and immediately began to harass college-aged young Black people who were part of the city's chapter of the Student Nonviolent Coordinating Committee (SNCC), a primarily college-student-led organization that had been at the vanguard of the national student civil rights movement since the early 1960s. SNCC national chairman Stokely Carmichael—who had coined the term "structural racism" the previous year—had turned the organization's focus from the South to the North and begun using the phrase "Black Power," calling for Black people to arm themselves if they wanted to defend themselves from police violence. Without evidence, Rizzo said local SNCC activists were "stockpiling" weapons so they could launch an attack on police in the city and ordered officers to raid four homes in North Philadelphia. The officers said they found sticks of dynamite, and Rizzo announced that the young people were planning to blow up Independence Hall. SNCC spokespeople said the police had planted the explosives, but Rizzo nevertheless charged four local SNCC leaders. The charges were dismissed due to lack of evidence, but following the targeted attack, SNCC shut down its operations in the city. Rizzo wasn't done. His next targets were not members of an organization, or even college students. They were middle and high school students peacefully protesting for change in their schools.

In November 1967, 3,500 Black students marched out of their

classrooms and schools in the City of Brotherly Love and converged at the School District of Philadelphia's headquarters. They were not protesting for or against desegregation, integration, or segregation. They accepted that they would not be attending integrated, or even desegregated, schools anytime soon, but if they were to be segregated, they demanded more Black teachers and the creation of Black studies classes, particularly in history and English. They also wanted schools to stop punishing students who refused to salute the flag or say the pledge of allegiance, because some students said they did not believe justice and liberty were concepts often beneficially applied to Black people in the United States. Cecil Moore, the head of the NAACP during the period when that organization was calling for the desegregation of Girard, was by then campaigning to become mayor of Philadelphia. Mark Shedd, the district superintendent, decided that, as a way of supporting the students' exploration of democracy and civic engagement, he would allow campaign workers from Moore's mayoral campaign to enter public high schools to talk with students. Thinking about power and politics with the radical members of Moore's mayoral campaign galvanized students, who began to organize Black Student Associations to collectively pressure the school district to listen to their demands. On November 10, students held an all-day demonstration to demand schools in the city offer a course in African American history. School administrators threatened the students with expulsion. The next day, community leaders stood outside Philadelphia's primarily Black high schools and encouraged students to leave school and attend the "Black student rally" at the Board of Education building the next day. When the day dawned, students from middle and high schools across the city walked, bused, biked, and drove to the rally. They marched toward the Board of Education building shouting "Black Power!" and "Black Studies!" By eleven a.m., more than three thousand protesters had assembled, and the rally organizers emphasized that they should remain peaceful.

Meanwhile, inside the building, Superintendent Shedd, who was sympathetic to the protesters, decided to meet with ten student representatives and asked Mattie Humphrey, a consultant to the Community Relations Service of the U.S. Justice Department, to act as a liaison between the district and the students. The gathered students were asked to select ten or so of their peers to negotiate for them. As discussions got under way, Shedd reached out to police department officials and asked them not to send uniformed officers to the demonstration, saying that if police officials felt they needed to be present, they could come dressed in civilian attire. However, at noon, Police Commissioner Frank Rizzo arrived with 350 officers. They showed up not only in uniform but in riot gear as Rizzo ordered the officers to attack, saying, "Get their black asses!" He led the charge into the crowd himself, baton swinging frantically in all directions. Shedd and others who were there characterized the ensuing violence as a "police riot." Judge Raymond Pace Alexander, a highly influential Black judge in the city, said of the incident, "The mere display of brute force with 300–400 armed police encircling youngsters—easily excited school children—will itself cause the explosion that occurred Friday afternoon."

The following evening, more than one thousand primarily white students, parents, and teachers representing a variety of organizations held a rally to protest police action. They gathered outside the Police Administration building. Some of the groups in attendance included Philadelphia Area Teachers for Peace, the Philadelphia Chapter of Students for a Democratic Society, Youth Against War and Fascism, and the South Philadelphia branch of the Consumers Education and Protection Association. A few of the Black student protesters addressed the crowd, and all who spoke denounced the actions of the police and called for Commissioner Rizzo to be at least disciplined, if not fired. Instead of getting fired, a few years later, in November 1971, Frank Rizzo was elected mayor of Philadelphia and expanded the list of causes he was against to include school desegregation, affirmative action, the desegregation of public housing, and other civil-rights-era programs he claimed gave "special privileges" to non-white people. These "special privileges" are also called citizenship rights and protections, and Black people continued to struggle mightily to obtain them in relation to education.

By this time, the ideas planted by Coleman and Moynihan had taken on a life of their own. In April 1969, Arthur Jensen, an educational psychologist at the University of California, Berkeley, published an article in the *Harvard Educational Review* in which he presented research on and popularized long-discredited pseudoscientific theories of Black inferiority. He argued that the achievement gap Coleman identified was due to innate, genetic differences in intelligence between white and Black students. Jensen went so far as to argue that Black people lacked even the rudimentary intelligence necessary for remedial education programs aimed at closing racial achievement gaps:

> There are intelligence genes, which are found in populations in different proportions, somewhat like the distribution of blood types. The number of intelligence genes seems to be lower, over-all, in the black population than in the white. As to the effect of racial mixing, nobody has yet performed experiments that reveal its relative effect on I.Q. If the racial mixture weren't there, it is possible that the I.Q. differences between blacks and whites would be even greater.

That is the lesson to be found in a 1973 front-page *Washington Post* story that opened with this analogy: "The doctors, you might say, keep telling the parents that their child's case is hopeless, that no amount of money or variety of remedies will add up to a cure." The accompanying image was a picture of a Black student in a remedial reading class. Jensen testified about his research discoveries at a congressional hearing in 1970 alongside scientists and public figures who opposed school integration. During his testimony, Jensen was careful to avoid explicitly supporting segregation; however, he warned that integration would lead to Black students being funneled into "normal" classes, rather than special classes for "the retarded," and that teachers would mistakenly "treat Black children like the average white child."

According to the Southern Poverty Law Center, prior to the publication of Jensen's article, the postwar scientific community had broadly debunked theories on racial differences because of "collective horror at Nazi atrocities, the generally widespread approval of the successes of the civil rights movement," and advances in genetic research that brought the very idea of "race" as a biological concept into dispute. Scientists and scholars had begun to see racial inequality as a sociological phenomenon resulting from centuries of discrimination and structural oppression rather than attributing it to innate differences between Black and white people. But Jensen's research, the Southern Poverty Law Center said, "became a catalyst for a racist backlash against that social scientifically backed consensus, a backlash fueled by Nixon-era policy decisions, and the actions of segregationists still bitter over their defeat 15 years earlier" in the 1954 *Brown v. Board of Education* Supreme Court decision. The national mood toward providing Black children a quality education was shifting, and in 1970 Daniel Moynihan told *Life* magazine that "the winds of Jensen were gusting through the capital at gale force."

This ideology, which became known as "Jensenism," validated the views of those interested in keeping schools segregated. Most concerning is that even attempts at reform were at their earliest stages of development influenced and driven by worries about pathology in Black communities. Harvard historian Elizabeth Hinton quotes the director of the education division of a New York City program called Mobilization for Youth as saying that the preschool classes that the organization offered to low-income families were designed to "head off retardation that most often comes early in these slum areas." She adds that in 1973, a St. Louis public school administrator boasted that a similar early education program at the highly segregated Benjamin Banneker Elementary School had successfully established "a middle-class environment in a slum neighborhood school" by giving the "deprived child" the tools to become "an able student and later a productive member of society."

Dr. Kenneth B. Clark, one of the psychologists whose research was cited in *Brown v. Board of Education,* was quoted in a *New York Times* article from 1972 as saying he firmly believed that these studies represented a "sophisticated type of backlash" to the *Brown* decision. Bemoaning what he believed were a rising number of social scientists "beclouding the issues," he pleaded for the courts and legislative bodies alone to decide questions of school spending and integration, "not on the basis of uncertain research findings," but based on the constitutional "equity rights of human beings." Black social scientists also spoke out against the conclusions of the Coleman and Moynihan reports and agreed with Dr. Clark's assessment that their work undermined Black progress, lamenting in a 1973 article in the *Harvard Educational Review*, "In recent years public perspective on American social science has been dominated by a species of inquiry most notably characterized by the published works of Coleman and Moynihan."

Less than two decades after *Brown,* the clashing hopes and fears of integration had given way to the promulgation of the worst stereotypes about Black people by white segregationists intent on repelling Black people from their schools. Coleman's and Moynihan's studies gave scientific credence to and made mainstream the idea that the issues Black children and their families faced were self-perpetuated, while Jensen planted and disseminated the idea that racist white people were right in thinking that Black people were inherently dirty, dumb, and prone to criminality. This sort of thinking soon become central to educational policy.

In the aftermath of a party or celebration, there are only two ways to dispose of balloons. You can pop them and get them to the trash as quickly as possible, or you can just leave them and wait for the slow decline, as the air leaks out over days. With the latter method, no matter how round and full it is blown, or how meaningful and remarkable the occasion, over time the balloon slowly shrinks and sags to a shriveled remain until, at last, it is a sad piece of trash to be tossed and forgotten. This is one of the more disheartening images I carry around as I think about the space between the "before times" of educational segregation when, as lived by my grandparents, education was meant to broadly prepare the majority of Black children for lives living, working, and being predominantly with other Black people and the "after times," or slow deflation, decay, and ruin that followed *Brown* as it relates to the role and presence of Black teachers and schools. My father saw, heard, and felt the hiss and shrink as the air of justice and educational support left the balloon of integration that was to have lifted Black children up and out of second-class citizenship. My father and *Roundabout* were part of the transition.

Until now, I have never really told stories about my father. People sometimes asked me what he was like. I found ways to avoid answering. I think some may have ended up thinking he had maybe been absent for much of my life, someone who wandered out for milk one day and never came back. It wasn't true. I knew him as well as he would let me when we were together, which was somewhere between regularly and often. It's just I never told stories about my father. I tell some pretty good stories about my father's side of the family. Like about how my cousin Bessie got "happy" in church and was feeling the spirit something fierce until her "we didn't know it was one" wig fell off. She got "unhappy" so fast that, for a bit, I didn't think God spoke clearly to folks with hairpieces. I could make a dinner party howl with laughter imitating how my grandma Isabelle, who, when she was fussing with her husband, my uncle Bill, could croak out and hurl snatches of church hymns at him in a way that turned traditional praise songs into sharply honed weapons of psychological destruction. I talked about my family all the time—just not my father.

There were no gut-wrenchingly horrible tales about abandonment, neglect, or abuse of any kind. No side-achingly funny stories about the time he did so and so. He never starred in any telling little anecdotes about being Black/male/heterosexual/middle-class/southern in the United States. There were no tales that twisted hearts or misted eyes. I never made him fairy-tale perfect, or nightmarishly frightening, neither Bigger Thomas tragic nor Teacake sweet. He just wasn't a character in the stories I told others. It's not that I didn't know anything about him. I often think about telling the story of the time he ruined his new Volkswagen Beetle, purchased by proud parents to celebrate his acceptance to law school. He told me he drove it near the ocean's edge at low tide and watched it as the waves crept closer, and the tide rose higher. He wanted to see if the advertisements were true, and the car could float. He learned that they did float! But he also found that after the Volkswagen's body proved itself seaworthy, the car's engine protested the experiment, refusing to work again. He was like that. He was curiosity and disinterest woven together. He was worthy of stories. I had some. I just didn't tell them. This remained true until the day I found myself scrolling through a newspaper article about a War on Poverty–era televised educational experiment aimed at Black children who lived in urban areas, and I saw that the show's host had my father's name.

And so, it turned out that long after his death, my father had a story to tell me. His story helps me explain how leaders in the federal government went from viewing educational integration as the best way to make good on the nation's citizenship promise to Black people to, by the 1970s, absolving themselves of responsibility for educational inequality and making Black people a problem to be feared, ignored, and policed. Where once the idea of Black school teachers and schools was to educate as many Black children as possible to a variety of social stations, the cure of integration left the educational body weak, barely alive, and angry. This is what was happening in the country when my mother decided I should attend a low-resourced, high-poverty, segregated middle school in San Francisco where there were no white students—though, in addition to Black people there were Samoans, Filipinos, and Chicanos. We were all undereducated and overpoliced together.

UNDEREDUCATED AND OVERPOLICED

n 1968, the year Martin Luther King was murdered, my parents determined neither would be happy in life if married to each other. They divorced when I was five. They had met and married in San Francisco, where my mother migrated from Center Point, Arkansas, with my grandma Isabelle and her husband, whom I grew up calling Uncle Bill. My father was in San Francisco attending law school. This divorce-induced splitting of families is part of how I grew up feeling and understanding home. Water was a constant. From oceans to bays and rivers, water was everywhere in both places. In Florida, there was a certain way water impregnated the air, making it heavy enough to settle on the head and shoulders with the weight of a shawl in summer. It was called humidity. The chilly version of air and water I felt in San Francisco was called fog. Living between two different cultures, family dynamics, and forms of water in the 1970s–'80s, I experienced most of the educational equity strategies the nation then had on offer. My educational experiences taught me lessons about how education could help lead to social and economic advancement and how it could make such advancement impossible.

The custody arrangement my parents came up with involved my

spending one school year with my father and grandparents in Clear-water and the next year with my mother, who traveled around a bit for my first few years of education. In an educational sense, though some years are hazy, what I remember is that I attended an almost brand-new Head Start program as a four-year-old in Clearwater; first grade in Washington, D.C., where my mother worked for a few years at what was then called Federal City College; third grade in Clearwater at a Catholic school in town; and fourth grade at a school named Le Conte Elementary, populated by Black and Spanish-speaking children, in the overwhelmingly Chicano Mission District neighborhood in San Francisco. In the fifth grade, I rode a yellow school bus to desegregate an overwhelmingly white school in Pinellas County, Florida, during the early 1970s, when the county law forbade any school from having fewer than 70 percent white students. In the sixth grade, just as federal education policies shifted from a focus on schools as central for racial balancing and resource sharing to halting the supposed spread of juvenile delinquency, I was back in San Francisco at Potrero Hill Middle School. By then, politicians had decided that schools were no longer a place to solve problems but rather a mechanism to separate and contain the children who social scientists said were causing all the issues.

In many ways, I think my educational journey began when I was a third grader in Catholic school. One day, two seemingly college-aged white people came into the classroom, pulled me out, and said that my teacher had recommended that they give me a test to see if I should take some special classes. I don't remember exactly how much time passed before I was told I had been identified as a "gifted" student. This is a designation familiar to many Black people who successfully desegregated and were accepted at predominantly white schools. I can't speak to other people, but in my case, my designation had to do with the fact that my grandmother had taught me to read early in life, so the test for entry into the gifted program was easy for me. It merely required reading pages from a *Dick and Jane* book at a time when I was already reading much heftier fare. Though at the time I didn't know it was important, for the next few years of my educational career, the "gifted" label followed me like a shield or letter of introduction. It meant that, unlike many of the Black peers with whom I was bused to our newly integrated school, I was placed into smaller, more advanced classes, which offered extra attention and a bit more support. And since there was usually just one of me, my presence frightened no one. I didn't feel like an invasion to the parents and administrators. Unlike what was true for so many Black children, educational "tracking," which in the seventies was used to undereducate generations of Black children by placing them into lower-performing classes at their newly desegregated and integrated schools, benefited me, because I was identified early as deserving enhanced academic opportunity. I got used to being in smaller classes with smiling teachers and helpful administrators. I took it for granted.

All that changed once I walked through the doors of the high-poverty, racially segregated neighborhood middle school I attended in San Francisco in 1975. The only time I have ever found myself in the back of a police car was during the year I attended that school. The first time an adult told me I was not smart enough to go to college was at that school. The first time I found myself surrounded by a group of peers chanting "fight, fight, fight" was in that school. The only time I tried to physically fight a teacher was in that school. I'm not sure who I would have become if I had stayed in that economically and racially segregated public school for longer than a year. I became someone who traveled an educational path that felt like a journey from encouraged to discouraged.

The fight for racial integration in San Francisco schools has a long history, with efforts first beginning in the early nineteenth century. Starting in 1830, free, freed, and self-emancipated Black people pushed hard against inequality in the city, organizing state and national citizenship conventions to strategize on how to achieve educational, labor, and legal justice. By 1853, at one of these meetings, a statewide commit-tee of Black men decided to spearhead a campaign to repeal an 1852 law barring Black children from taxpayer-supported common schools. As a result of their efforts, for a limited period in the 1850s, some school dis-tricts in California admitted Black children to common schools with white students, but it was infrequent, and sometimes their stay in these white classrooms was short-lived. In 1854, for instance, when the Grass Valley Common School first opened, there were three Black children enrolled. But after about a week, one of the white students mentioned the Black students' presence to their parents, who immediately peti-tioned district officials to have the Black children removed and the school formally designated as white only. The school's trustees refused the request but forwarded the petition on to the state superintendent of public instruction, who ordered the trustees to exclude the Black children or lose their state funding. The trustees again refused because, they said, the law allowed for integrated classrooms.

In response, the legislature moved to amend the school segregation laws, and after 1859, neither Black, Chinese, nor Indigenous children could legally attend school with white children in California. In 1864, the state superintendent of public schools, John Swett, in his *Thir-teenth Annual Report,* said there were 831 Black school-age children in California and six state-supported "colored schools" located in San Francisco, Sacramento, Marysville, San Jose, Stockton, and Petaluma. These schools could serve only a fraction of the Black children in the state. Black people not near one of those six areas and schools did not have access to free public schools. If they wanted their children to be educated, Black families had to find the money to pay private school fees themselves. White children in the state, however, had universal access to free education.

In November 1871, at a Black citizenship convention held in Stockton, California, called for the purpose of discussing the lack of educational options in the state, those attending adopted a resolution to petition the legislature to remove the words "children of African descent" from the law so Black children could "be allowed educational facilities with other children." Following the convention, Senator Seldon J. Finney of San Mateo County took up the cause and introduced a bill in the California legislature to end racial segregation in schools. The bill failed. The next step took place in 1872, when Black leaders decided to pursue a test case in court.

At the time, San Francisco had two "colored schools" located at opposite ends of the city, one of which was only a small room rented by the Board of Education. According to an article in a local Black newspaper called *The Appeal,* white children had access to "43 or more splendidly built schoolhouses in the city suited or adapted to every neighborhood." On July 23, 1872, *The San Francisco Chronicle* reported that several Black parents had attempted to enroll their children in different white schools but had been denied, and that an attorney was planning to litigate the case on their behalf. One of those parents was Harriet Ward, who had tried to register her eleven-year-old daughter, Mary Frances, at the public school closest to her home. The principal, Noah Flood, refused to allow Mary to enroll, advising Ward that she should take Mary to one of the "colored schools." The case went to the California State Supreme Court, which ruled in 1874 that "separate but equal" schools for Black students were legal. This was twenty-two years before the U.S. Supreme Court reached the same conclusion for the entire nation in *Plessy v. Ferguson.*

Black children were not alone in being educated in segregated environments. The first segregated public school for Chinese children opened in 1859 and operated until 1870, when the school district closed it, determining that Chinese students were ineligible to attend any public schools in the city, segregated or not. In a frenzy of anti-immigrant sentiment, the state used public education as a weapon to punish them for being foreign-born. Public education remained unavailable to them for fifteen years. In 1885, parental protest and activism in the Chinese American community lead the California Supreme Court to decide that, as residents of the state, Chinese students had a right to attend public schools. In response to the ruling, instead of putting them in schools with white students, SFUSD reopened the segregated Chinese school that had closed in 1870, renaming it the "Oriental School." Chinese students had the right to attend school, but not with white children. As anti-Asian integration sentiment continued to harden, beginning in 1906, Japanese and Korean immigrant children who had previously been classified as white in the school district, and so attended schools with white students, were now reclassified as "Oriental" and required to attend the one school in the city now designated for all Asian children.

This renewed commitment to Asian segregation sparked an international incident, because the Japanese government said the school board's edict violated an 1894 treaty providing Japanese residents in the United States the same rights as white American citizens. President Theodore Roosevelt soon became embroiled in the controversy. In his annual message to Congress, he chided the city for putting his foreign policy objectives with Japan at risk, describing the school board's action as a "wicked absurdity" and adding that a city "should not be allowed to commit a crime against a friendly nation." Newspapers in Japan publicized what was happening to Japanese families in San Francisco and inflamed Japanese public opinion against the school district and the United States. President Roosevelt defused the situation and placated people in both Japan and San Francisco through an informal agreement in which the district rescinded its segregation policy for Japanese students and, in return, Japan promised to deny visas to laborers seeking to immigrate to the United States. For Black children, who were increasingly barred from public schools in California and did not have foreign governments to apply pressure on their behalf, church-based private schools were a common way for them to get an education.

This sort of educational exclusion based on race remained in place for decades. Finally, in San Francisco in 1947, Chicano families won a legal battle against school segregation, arguing that their children deserved unqualified access to public schools. Two months later, Governor Earl Warren, who would almost a decade later preside over the *Brown* case as a Supreme Court justice, signed a bill ending legal school segregation of any kind in California, making it the first state in the country to do so. Legally segregated schools were a thing of the past in San Francisco, yet there were no district-wide attempts to ensure equal and widespread access to the wealthier schools in the city. As a result, segregation and discrimination, though no longer legal, continued, especially against Black, Indigenous, and Latino students. It would take the district more than two decades to come up with an actual plan to try to desegregate all its schools. It wasn't by choice. The courts began to force change.

In 1971, following years of organizing by the San Francisco branch of the NAACP, the U.S. District Court ruled that the San Francisco Unified School District violated the law by *intentionally* drawing segregated student assignment zones and assigning Black teachers only to majority-Black schools. It also found that teachers in segregated Black schools were systematically less experienced and more poorly paid compared to teachers in San Francisco's majority-white schools. After the court ruling, Thomas Shaheen, the new superintendent who had arrived in San Francisco a year earlier determined to right educational wrongs, helped launch a massive busing program within the San Francisco Unified School District. The goal of the "Horseshoe Plan," named thus because of its shape on the map, was to integrate forty-eight thousand students in ninety-seven elementary schools. This plan was unusually complicated, calling for students to spend half of their elementary school years walking to a school close to home and the other half being bused to a different school within their zone. This meant children would attend two different schools and arrive at the schools in two different ways during one school year.

Opinion polls at the time made clear that families of all racial groups disliked busing as a desegregation strategy, but white and Asian families were the least supportive of SFUSD's overall desegregation goal. There was no violence involved or even protests, but scattered boycotts by white and Chinese parents meant only around twenty-nine thousand children were in class on the day schools were set to integrate. Almost 40 percent of students, overwhelmingly white and Chinese, were absent. Reporters who watched buses leave Chinatown told the *New York Times* that they were all virtually empty. One had a lone passenger. Another strong pocket of boycott resistance to busing was on Treasure Island, a Navy base where no one lives but Navy personnel. They opposed having their children bused, and that previous month, Navy Secretary John H. Chafee had said that the school district should reconsider busing plans altogether.

These communities largely (though not uniformly) fought for access to neighborhood schools that their children could walk to and attend over the whole year. White parents began to pull their children out of the system in protest, and the white population in schools decreased by 11 percent in the first year of the desegregation plan and continued to drop over the next decade. Chinese student enrollment also decreased by 8 percent in the first year of the plan but leveled off in following years. White flight in San Francisco was among the most pronounced in the country—more than twenty thousand white students left SFUSD following the implementation of desegregation, the third-largest exodus behind only Atlanta and Detroit. As a result of this white and, to a lesser extent, Chinese resistance to the desegregation plan, Black families became increasingly frustrated as it became clear that desegregation in San Francisco would function as a one-way system that took their children to schools outside their neighborhood without students from other racial groups being bused into theirs. This was a complaint gaining in volume around the country.

By the 1970s, all over the United States the idea of busing, desegregation, and affirmative action, designed to desegregate K–12 schools as well as colleges for Black and other non-white students, led to backlash from white people who had come to believe they were being discriminated against. Sometimes these responses turned violent, like when in 1970 a mob of two hundred white people attacked buses carrying thirty-five Black schoolchildren on their way to integrate predominantly white schools in Lamar, South Carolina. The next year, in Pontiac, Michigan, six members of the Ku Klux Klan were indicted for planting dynamite with the goal of blowing up buses Black children were meant to board to desegregate schools in the area. Instead of denouncing such acts of domestic terrorism by white racists against Black children and communities, when speaking of the mood of the country, President Nixon was overheard on White House recordings from the Oval Office saying to his chief of staff, H. R. Haldeman, "You have to face the fact that the whole problem is really the Blacks. The key is to devise a system that recognizes this while not appearing to." In other words, white people weren't to be blamed for vehemently and violently opposing racial integration and violating the law; Black families and children were to be blamed for both wanting laws followed and for wanting a quality education. President Nixon successfully exploited race-based experiences with and anxieties about school integration during his reelection campaign.

Soon after taking office in 1969, Nixon dropped the government's plans to withhold funds from southern school districts that remained segregated—a plan that had been leading southern school systems to finally desegregate—and backed southern attempts to postpone the 1970 deadline for the abolition of all segregated schools. As Dartmouth historian Matt Delmont has noted, this was the first time since the 1954 *Brown* decision that a presidential administration openly sided with segregationists. But despite these actions, as the 1972 presidential elections approached, Nixon found that his campaign might not have completely locked up the white segregationist vote. One of his main opponents, a former governor of Alabama, George Wallace, was already very popular with voters who did not want school integration or desegregation, and unlike Nixon, Wallace had a history of putting his body on the line to keep educational institutions primarily white, as demonstrated by his rallying cry for "Segregation now. Segregation tomorrow. Segregation forever" at the University of Alabama in 1963. Almost ten years later, during his presidential run in 1972, he turned his known resistance to desegregation into a campaign issue, telling voters his earlier views remained intact and promising them that if he were elected, he would support a national moratorium on all busing aimed at bringing about racial integration in public schools.

If he was going to successfully compete against Wallace and be reelected, Nixon determined that he would have to do more to make clear he was both against busing and would not be enforcing school integration policies. This was a sound strategy because busing was unpopular not only among southern racists or conservatives, but also among many northern white people and politicians who considered themselves moderates or liberals. White parents who had moved out of cities to escape sending their children to school with non-white children did not want to have to think about accepting Black children into the schools their tax dollars supported. Nixon campaigned hard on his opposition to busing, assuring his supporters and voters on the fence about voting for him that, without federal support for busing, Black schoolchildren could not integrate into suburban schools and that rather than being bused, white children could remain in their overwhelmingly white neighborhood schools.

According to John Ehrlichman, Nixon's domestic affairs adviser, Nixon's "political compass told him to stay away from the whole subject of race." But he added that Nixon and his advisers believed that, if he could not completely avoid talking about race, the best political course for him would be to make clear that he was "on the side of the white parents whose children were about to get on those hated buses." Nixon won reelection handily, and in 1972 he proposed the Equal Educational Opportunities Act to direct more federal funding to inner-city urban schools. He didn't use the words, but in effect Nixon relied on the logic of separate but equal that the *Brown v. Board* decision had overturned in 1954. Dr. Delmont summarizes Nixon's actions this way: "The compromise Nixon offered was quite explicit: students in the city would remain in the city and not be permitted to attend suburban schools; in exchange for staying put, they would get more resources." It was a compromise that responded to white fears about public policies that supported racial integration at the literal educational expense of urban communities. Two years after starting his post, in 1972, Shaheen was asked to resign by Mayor Joseph Alioto for pressing ahead too far and too fast in his calls for full integration of schools in the city, and for accusing the San Francisco Board of Education of trying to "run a private school system for the white community."

Though I wouldn't begin sixth grade until the fall of 1975, Potrero Hill Middle School opened in August 1971, at the height of the lawsuits and tensions over integration, busing, and racism in San Francisco public schools. School officials, when planning for demographics, paid special attention to racial balance and devised a busing program that would yield a student body that was 44 percent Black, 26 percent Latino, and 22 percent white at the school. There were no plans to bus Chinese students. Chinese parents bitterly and successfully resisted busing plans in the city and attempted to have their children exempted, with some making plans to open private schools where Chinese students would learn Cantonese and traditional Chinese culture. This was necessary, they said, because if they were forced to comply with desegregation plans, "the cultural and educational life of the Chinese community in San Francisco will, as a practical matter, be destroyed."

One of the organizers of the private school said, "If you're giving better education by this busing situation, I'm for it, but if you can't, leave my children at home." Another Chinese parent used the de facto segregation argument to justify the community's opposition to busing. "We don't have a colored problem," they said, explaining—under the assumption all Black people were too poor to move into wealthy neighborhoods where the schools were better—that "it's too expensive for them. The prices of these houses are too high." Rather than engage in the Asian version of white flight, the parent said, "Here we will make our stand. If you whites can't stop this thing, we Chinese will stop it."

The construction of Potrero Hill Middle School, the first middle school in the area and within walking distance for neighborhood kids, had been approved by the school board in 1964, but controversies over siting for the school, protest from residents who would be displaced by school construction, spiraling budget estimates, and a refusal to include any non-white members on the planning committee doomed the project to constant postponement. Black community members whose children would comprise the majority of students at the school decried the lack of input they were allowed. As it turns out, this exclusion was intentional, and a representative of the Potrero Hill Boosters and Merchants, one of the groups consulted about demographics and census, said the larger community did not need to be invited to planning meetings because "This is not going to be a ghetto school." The lack of Black community input was further amplified when Black parents discovered that Thomas Shaheen, the short-lived school superintendent, had chosen a white principal for the school when there had been well-qualified Black applicants with experience working in schools that were predominantly non-white. John Sammon, the new principal, did in fact have experience working with Black children, most recently as the principal at a majority-Black school in the Bayview–Hunters Point area of San Francisco, but had been reassigned after two and a half years due to charges that he was ill-equipped to lead an institution full of Black children.

In December 1971, a group calling themselves the Potrero Hill Legal Defense Fund penned an angry letter to Superintendent Shaheen accusing him of disrespecting Black parents. They described themselves as a group organized to support schools in addressing the needs of community youth. The letter asked, "Tell us about Democracy, Mr. Shaheen? Supposedly you picked the man who was best qualified . . . best qualified for what and for whom?" The letter posited that Shaheen's "definition of 'qualified' has little to do with the people, the community or the actual work the principal will have to perform." They found it particularly upsetting that he would be chosen over Black candidates to lead another school full of Black and Chicano students after he had been forced out of his previous school. They warned the superintendent that if he did not listen to them, they would be forced to "Work hard to remove your pests as rapidly as you breed them."

Their concerns were ignored, and Sammon would end up being appointed anyway. In a YouTube video from 2015 featuring a discussion between four white men who were among the first group of teachers hired at Potrero Hill Middle School—one of whom came to teaching after retiring from the police department—the participants lauded the principal. One said that because the school board superintendent had given Mr. Sammon free rein to hire whomever he wanted, the school had been full of many bright and enthusiastic teachers. Though they had abundant energy, the speaker also notes that few came to their post with teaching experience. As I watched the short clip, I was struck by the white teachers' praise for Sammon's decision to saddle children who were behind academically and needed attention with inexperienced white teachers who knew little about either them or their communities. Their assessment was notably different from what Black parents told the press at the time.

In the spring of 1972, a few years before I began attending the school, the *Potrero View* ran a story with the headline "Violence at the Junior High School," in response to what was described as a growing number of personal attacks, thefts, and threatening behavior of the students toward each other as well as teachers and administrators. The article described a parent-teacher town hall in which the overwhelmingly white teaching force complained about how poorly prepared they were to handle the students and how, other than suspension and removal from school, there were not a lot of good options for doing so. The white teachers in attendance said that racism had nothing to do with the rapidly devolving situation in the school. There were only two Black teachers in attendance at the meeting, and the small number of parents there were agitated because, since the chair of the meeting would not allow the Black teachers to freely participate in the discussion, the assurances of the white teachers that racism was nowhere to be found went unchallenged. Those teachers who were allowed to speak suggested that the discipline of the Black students at the school should potentially be broadened to include corporal punishment, which was illegal at the time, and the increased use of suspensions and detentions. One of the Black parents in attendance said that there needed to be people in positions of authority at the school who understood the world in which the students in public housing had learned to live, where it was crucial to learn how to fight and defend themselves as soon as they were old enough to go outside without an adult.

It wasn't just the adults who were concerned about fighting. In May 1973, given the levels of violence that continued at the school unabated, a few students got together and decided to conduct a poll of some eighth-grade students to gather their opinions. On the question of crime and student discipline, they expressed strong support for more discipline, or anything that would help them feel safe. The students mentioned having their hair pulled or witnessing classmates who overturned others' trays in the cafeteria, hit students, and just generally "messed everything up." They wished their peers had more respect for "other people's property" and didn't think they should be allowed to run around the halls when they were supposed to be in class. Because the neighborhood was so heavily poor and of color, white students from the army base at Treasure Island were bused in, and the types of violence described included beating up the children from Treasure Island, setting fires in the bathrooms, and using open locker doors as a weapon. When asked what they would change, they said there needed to be more respect for the rights of students who wanted protection from violence.

I wish I could say I disagreed with their assessment, but what I remembered from my sixth-grade experience was strikingly like what these students recalled. By the time I enrolled at Potrero in 1975, "Operation Integrate," which had been launched by the school district a year earlier, had expanded the previous desegregation plan to middle and high schools in SFUSD. Potrero first began with seventh and eighth graders, but by 1975 when I matriculated there, they had added sixth graders. Though one benefit of attending the school was that it was a relatively short walk from my house, it was a school with few windows, so students couldn't see out and the outside world could not see in. This was also the exact moment when politicians were beginning to embrace and legislate for the idea that poor children of color in urban schools weren't likely to succeed in school no matter how well funded they were. The only real plan for educating such children, integration/desegregation, had fallen completely off the public policy stage, and controlling and containing Black children rose to fill the space.

With the passage of the Juvenile Justice and Delinquency Prevention Act in 1974, the federal government officially shifted from managing the symptoms of urban poverty through programs like Head Start and television shows like *Roundabout* or *Sesame Street* to a strategy centered on expanding the power of the Justice Department in schools, especially those serving children and teenagers in segregated urban communities, to manage "juvenile delinquency."

As Elizabeth Hinton explores in her history of the rise of policing in schools in the 1970s, the newly formed Office of Juvenile Justice and Delinquency Prevention gave the federal government dominion over issues of crime and violence in urban public schools, public housing, and low-income neighborhoods. In the summer of 1974, when Congress renewed the Secondary Education Act—which outlined federal aid guidelines for elementary and secondary schools—it introduced new funding for widespread police patrols in the hallways and classrooms of schools serving low-income children. Less than a year after the passage of this legislation, officials in the Ford administration proposed various techniques to further increase surveillance and patrol of low-income students by combining electronic surveillance, improved security of school buildings, and a greater law enforcement presence on the campuses of urban public schools. A former New York City public school teacher, Congresswoman Shirley Chisholm, made her colleagues aware of the connections between youth crime and school disciplinary measures in hearings addressing juvenile delinquency held by the Subcommittee on Equal Opportunity. "When school systems are not able to cope with the uniqueness and specific needs of Black children," Chisholm explained, "we find the development of discipline problems."

By the time I arrived at Potrero, there were police all over the school. They mostly seemed disinterested. Their disinterest mirrored that of teachers who did not seem to be there to guide and protect. I learned early that it was not a good idea to carry books in the hallways. Doing so made you a target for ridicule, or maybe even attack. I learned to avoid the bathrooms completely or enter in a group to avoid physical or sexual assault. For the first time in my life, I attended a school where the teachers didn't bother to interact with us or learn our names. They handed out worksheets and sat quietly as we worked on them, or didn't work on them, or talked to our neighbor for the whole class. I cut school one day with a friend who took me downtown and taught me to shoplift. I was terrible at it, got caught, and ended up in the back of a police car. As I headed to the station, I considered whether there was any universe in which I could keep from having to call my mother for help. The officers let us go, because it was the end of their shift, but I later learned—as did my mother—that the police had notified the school and advised that I be considered at high risk for juvenile delinquency. Because this all took place at the exact time when the federal government had begun to intertwine schooling with policing, that one moment could have ended up very differently.

The Horseshoe Plan and Operation Integrate worked initially, especially at reducing Black–white segregation. But despite these efforts, because neighborhoods remained segregated and busing remained unpopular, schools continued to be segregated by race at the start of the 1976–77 school year. In response to white flight and community resistance, the SFUSD went back to the drawing board and this time proposed a new student assignment plan called "Educational Redesign" to fix the problem. It adopted a policy of "racial unidentifiability," requiring every school to enroll students from at least four racial/ ethnic groups, with no one group exceeding 45 percent of total enrollment. Middle-class white and Asian families supported the new plan, in part to keep their children from being required to attend school outside their neighborhoods.

A strategy fully and equitably funding high-quality schools in all neighborhoods, even if they are of color or poor, is a strategy that we in the United States have rarely tried. Embracing separate but equal education would bring increased and targeted resources to schools in Black communities with a focus on meeting the needs of these students. This focus would view Black communities not as inferior communities, but as communities deprived of equitable resources necessary for the delivery of quality education. And therein lies the dilemma: Do you attempt to dilute the inherent, unequal nature of segregation and eliminate the effects of the legacy of education denial by bringing a racial balance to school districts? Or do you allow people to live within the safety of their comfort zones and provide communities with the resources and stabilizing policies they have been historically denied?

There is, of course, evidence of the efficacy of the former. As I've noted, our nation's earlier efforts at desegregation led to significant gains in academic attainment levels for some Black students, along with many other societal improvements. "Racial achievement gaps declined substantially during the 1970s and 1980s, providing evidence that desegregation could reduce inequality in educational outcomes," read a 2019 report from the Stanford Center for Education Policy Analysis. "Studies of the effects of the desegregation of southern school districts during this time show that desegregation had a positive impact on Black students and no negative impact on white students." A report from the National Bureau of Economic Research also found that "southern-born Blacks who finished their schooling just before effective desegregation occurred in the South fared poorly compared to southern-born Blacks who followed behind them in school by just a few years." On the other hand, our nation's failed efforts at desegregation, coupled with an inability to offer Black students public schools that supported them, caused undeniable harm to Black communities. As the noted playwright of *Raisin in the Sun,* Lorraine Hansberry, explained in a 1965 speech to writers from the *Monthly Review:*

> Black folk in America have historically regarded education with reverence. All the more poignant and ugly, then, that the withholding of education has been one of the prime instruments of the oppressors of American Negroes—oppressors who have seen to it that even when education could not be entirely withheld it could certainly be made substandard.

A product of Chicago's system herself, Hansberry told the crowd that her experience with America's racially segregated, overcrowded schools in the 1960s taught her what it felt like to be educated by disinterested teachers in overcrowded classrooms, not to be respected and loved. Despite tests showing she was considered gifted, "To this day, I do not add, subtract, or multiply with ease. . . . This is what we mean when we speak of the scars, the marks that the ghettoized child carries through life. . . . To be imprisoned in the ghetto is at best to be forgotten, or at most to be deliberately cheated out of one's birthright."

By the time I enrolled at Potrero Hill Middle School, Black teachers organizing to ensure their children were protected was central to the politics of cities in the United States. Throughout the twentieth century, and continuing into the twenty-first, Black people in cities like Chicago, Oakland, Philadelphia, and Detroit, many of whom had migrated out of the South and had been taught by the sorts of southern teachers who so ably bolstered the self-concepts of their students, continued to organize to try to ensure that the demise of desegregation efforts did not mean the demise of quality education for Black children in the United States. They called for community control of schools and advocated for experimental schooling models. They also started their own schools to try to intervene in the continuing undereducation of Black children in the North.

Ericka Huggins, one of the founding members of the Black Panther Party chapters in Los Angeles and New Haven, Connecticut, became the director of the organization's Oakland Community School in 1973. It was a model for how to educate Black children from struggling urban areas. The school won awards for its innovative teaching and ability to turn undereducated students in urban public schools into successful students. The school grew out of point number five in the Black Panther Party's Ten-Point Program, which called for educating Black and poor people about their "true history" in the United States. Though Huggins often described the school as a model for education that was replicable anywhere, few schools were comparable to Oakland Community School, which educated Black children as young as two and a half. With most of the costs covered by donations, parents didn't have to pay much, if anything.

In 1976, the Alameda County Board of Supervisors gave Oakland Community School a special commendation for educational excellence, and in 1977 county lawmakers held a ceremony to recognize the Oakland Community School for its "highly effective service in educating children in the community of Oakland." Huggins's curriculum was innovative, and it won the school awards because it worked. Not only did students attending the school perform, on average, better than students enrolled in surrounding schools, but they were also taught according to an educational philosophy based on teaching children "how" more than "what" to think. Children learned meditation and yoga and were in classes with no more than ten students. Classes were organized by ability, not age. There were full periods on poetry writing, math, science, foreign languages, history, and current events. In addition, in terms of discipline, a child who misbehaved might be sent outside to meditate until he had calmed down, and a student board meted out discipline to their peers. Such interventions were rarely seen in traditional public schools. These were, however, widespread in the Black independent schools that flourished during the period I was in middle school in San Francisco. The continuing resistance to desegregation made it necessary.

In 1975, one particularly notable educator, Marva Collins, took $5,000 from her teacher's retirement fund and used the money to open a private school called Westside Preparatory School in Garfield Park, an urban area of Chicago. Collins began her career teaching in Alabama before moving to Chicago in 1959. She quickly became frustrated by both the conditions she saw in the segregated urban schools in which she taught and the overall low expectations of students held by both teachers and principals. Saying that she wanted the same education for all Black children as she wanted for her own, she opened her own school. Collins specifically recruited Black students to Westside Preparatory School who were poor and struggling academically, pointedly saying she was most interested in recruiting students to her school who were "dirty and smelly." She explained that "when children are poor, self-esteem and excellence are their ticket to being the very best." This was the gift she wanted to give to those students who she believed needed it the most. Both she and her methods proved so successful that, in 1980, President Ronald Reagan courted her to become secretary of education. She declined his offer. She thought she could do more in the classroom than as a government official. In 1988, as president-elect, President George H. W. Bush approached her again, asking that she consider setting education policy for the nation. Again, she declined.

Westside Prep was initially located on the top floor of the brownstone where she and her family lived. The school started out with only six students, four children from the neighborhood, plus her own two. In describing how she came up with her teaching techniques, she said she knew from fourteen years of teaching that students needed to read, write, and think, so those pursuits were at the core of her school's curriculum. In addition, she used the Socratic method and exposed them to the "great classics because they expose you to complex thought." Collins believed that the Chicago public school system simply refused to teach many Black children who were poor, instead labeling them as learning disabled. She said that one sure way to improve the education of and for Black children was to "stop talking about what's wrong with Black children who can't learn, because if you give them to me for a year, I guarantee you my last life I will give them back to you different children. I would love nothing more in my life than to show that there is nothing wrong with our children."

The students who graduated from Collins's Westside Prep received scholarships to Northwestern, Yale, and Harvard, and almost 90 percent graduated from college. She said her success was based on the strategies and pedagogy she had learned in Alabama when she attended segregated Black schools pre-*Brown*. She was patient, had high expectations, loved her students, found different ways to interest them in their lessons, and told them they could be and do anything. It was a simple yet successful strategy that bore bountiful fruit. Both integration and segregation educational strategies and policies have borne similar results. One offers an abundance of resources, while the other offers the psychic and emotional support that helps Black children thrive. One without the other can leave students in a state of deprivation or trauma. We know this firsthand from our son's experiences as he entered middle school in Princeton, New Jersey.

6

JELANI

O ver the course of my educational journey, both in schools that were middle-class and overwhelmingly white, as well as those full of majority-poor and Black- and brown-skinned people, I learned that schools produce predictable outcomes. I didn't start out in an underperforming, poor, and segregated school and discover the cleanliness and structured calm of integrated white schools. I started out in the latter, and only later in life stuck a toe into the wildly underfunded and overpoliced majority-Black educational ocean. That's where I learned that most Black children are barred from the types of school environments that would aid them in obtaining stable social and economic lives. My journey was different from my child's. He was never educated anywhere other than in integrated high-performing schools in Princeton, New Jersey. His educational journey carried him to completely different lands of understanding than did mine and affirms how, in the United States, class does not in fact function as some sort of kryptonite for anti-Blackness. Racism in education has long existed in both the South and the North and has always impacted middle- and upper-class Black people, as well as those who are poor or working-class. In schools like the ones my son attended, integration is wrapped up in educational inequality, if not violence. It's not easier to navigate the unequal policies and strategies in well-funded, integrated schools. It's just different.

Growing up in the overwhelmingly wealthy, white, and picturesque college town of Princeton, my son, Jelani, was for most of his childhood and adolescence the only Black child in many of his classes, and therefore his white friends' only Black friend. He was always popular, in part because he was easygoing, laughed often, and excelled at sports, but also because his parents were college professors. This meant that white parents felt comfortable having him in their homes for the ubiquitous sleepovers that began when he was in third grade, and with their children spending the night in ours. Jelani also had Black friends growing up, but they were rarely if ever as "accepted" in the intimate sense of being invited to share in the morning and evening family routines in the homes of his white friends.

His primary school years were for me an education in what Langston Hughes called "the ways of white folks." I had grown up with and around white students, parents, and people, but they were not close friends. And though education had always been something to be engaged in and taken seriously in my world, seeing each phase of the educational journey, starting in elementary school, as part of a strategy to get children into the most elite schools possible was new to me. The parents of Jelani's friends seemed to know how to ensure that their already advantaged children got into the classrooms with the "best" teachers, and the "best" students, and the "best" academic tracks. These parents were actively involved at each step and very focused on helping their children gain advantage by any means necessary.

I began to understand the full import of this lesson at one of the biannual elementary school open houses that parents and caretakers were regularly invited to attend. There, we met teachers and inspected our children's individual and group projects. On one of these nights, when Jelani was in the second or third grade, the students were tasked with creating dioramas and writing a presentation to explain their work. As was to be expected, the finished products varied in terms of skill or one being able to confidently identify what it was supposed to be. Jelani, like other children, had completed the assignment using shoeboxes, clay, and bits and pieces of plastic. But one child's father, an architect, had his staff build a small and modest, but operational, model of a house with battery-powered working lights. When it came time for the father/son duo to explain their work, the child just looked at his feet before seemingly pleading with his adult to speak in his stead. Dad obliged, and we all grinned and made a collective "aww" sound as he nudged his son forward to accept the polite applause. We all participated in the fiction that the shorter of the two presenters in front of us had accomplished something and congratulated the student for doing such a good job. This type of enthusiastic community support continued to be on offer to other students but was not regularly offered to our son in terms of academics, although given that he played a number of sports, he did receive community support for his skills in basketball, tennis, track, and soccer.

Though my husband and I were friendly with some of the parents of Jelani's friends, none clued us in on what was supposed to happen when our children approached the end of the fifth grade. Some of the white parents of children with standardized test scores outside the 95th percentile and therefore too low to guarantee placement on the middle school's "honors track" took drastic action. They hired lawyers and psychologists, and let administrators at the elementary school, middle school, and even school board know that should their child's placement not be to their liking, they were prepared to file formal complaints, provide evidence of special-needs accommodations, and, if necessary, file lawsuits to ensure their child's place in the most desirable classes. Many months later, I learned that this intensity about what classes our children took in the beginning of middle school was warranted, because these would determine our children's schedule in high school. The fight for math and science placement in the sixth grade was a move on a chessboard in which the winner was awarded with a course of study that would likely lead to acceptance at an elite college or university. Many of the other parents seemingly understood the significance of the sixth grade beyond the simple rite of passage that was leaving elementary school behind and beginning again at a higher level that was middle school. I didn't know the rules of this game and as a result could not play offense as effectively as I needed to. My rookie status explains how it came to be that my well-liked, academically talented twelve-year-old son left the fifth grade full of confidence and enthusiasm, only to enter a middle school that immediately labeled and treated him as an underachieving problem child.

It wasn't until Jelani had spent the first few weeks of the semester in his classroom doing worksheets and socializing with friends in his lower-level math and science classes that I came to understand that a mistake had been made. At the first student-teacher conference, his math teacher explained to all of us parents in the room that the class our children were in could not lead them to an Ivy League school. Most of us in the room were not white. Once the teacher explained the criteria for being placed in one of the higher classrooms, I asked about the process for getting our child moved, since he met or exceeded all of them. Assured that an honest mistake had been made, we filled out the requested paperwork and waited for change to come. Weeks passed, but nothing happened. We filed more paperwork and had a series of meetings with teachers, administrators, and members of the school board. Still, nothing changed. The last straw for us was when the Black principal at the school told us that parents often overestimated their children's skills and abilities and that perhaps we should just let Jelani stay on the remedial track where he had been placed in error, and which would dictate the options he would have to attend college. The principal told us, "School is hard. I wouldn't want to go through it again." I don't honestly know what he meant by this. I didn't bother asking. We knew we would be finding a new school for Jelani.

By then, we were done being patient and threatened the school board, not with a lawsuit, but rather with media attention to expose the inexplicable academic placement of Black students at the middle school. We said we were more than willing to make public the unsupportive actions of individual teachers and the lengths Black parents were forced to go through to correct what everyone assured us was merely an administrative error. That did get results. Jelani's placement was changed. Soon after, I ran into one of his white teachers at the grocery store. Looking around nervously, she said that if we at all could, we needed to figure out how to get Jelani out of the public school system. If we didn't, she said, we would "lose him." She said that the teachers in his school described him as arrogant and assured each other he was not as smart as his parents thought. She said feelings were hardening against him. One teacher accused Jelani of plagiarizing a five-paragraph essay, or of having his college professor parents write it for him.

He demanded that Jelani write an essay in class with him watching. Jelani complied and wrote an essay that one of the school employees told us was better than the one he had done at home. Instead of calming the controversy, his passing that one hurdle seemed to further enrage some. By the time the teacher warned us that she didn't know if he could survive the antipathy of her peers and urged us to find and pay for a private school to educate him if we could, we understood we were fighting forces we couldn't quite see. We were already looking at private schools, an option we hadn't planned for, and though the two of us had a combined salary that placed us solidly in the middle class, the price tag for private schools in the area had us scratching our heads trying to figure out how we would afford it.

Sociologists Jon Diamond and Amanda Lewis explore many of the issues with which we were faced in their 2015 book, *Despite the Best*

Intentions: How Racial Inequality Thrives in Good Schools, which talks
about how common this type of thing is in suburban schools. They
describe how racial inequality is produced

> . . . through tracking processes and processes of informal commu-
> nication amongst parents. Certain parents get access to the teach-
> ers who have the best reputations, and they make sure that the
> educational tracks privilege their children in terms of the resources
> allocated. District folks are pressured to provide the best educa-
> tion possible to the children whose parents they perceive as having
> the most power and the loudest voices. That situation is detrimen-
> tal to a large percentage of young people who don't have that kind
> of access.

As was true in our home, Black parents in these types of high-
performing districts are often unaware that this type of access and support is necessary. There was glue we could feel but not quite see sticking
Jelani in place in a classroom where he didn't belong. Its stickiness had
as much to do with the views of teachers and administrators in his present as it did with the school district's past with segregation, discomfort
with integration, and historical and contemporary difficulties educating Black children, be they rich or poor. It was a link in the historical
chain of massive resistance to schools accepting and equitably educating Black children.

Princeton High School first ran afoul of the federal No Child Left
Behind laws, which required public school districts to educate Black
and other children equally as measured by standardized test scores,
in 2004. Until that law, the federal government did not impose any
consequences on districts that failed to show they could educate all
children similarly across racial differences. That year, Princeton High
School received a failing mark because of the lagging scores of Black
students on a standardized English test given to eleventh graders. The

district was placed on probation. A year later, in 2005, the federal government cited the school for the second year in a row. This time, the infraction was the fact that 37 percent of Black students failed to meet standards in English, and 55 percent of Black and 40 percent of Latino students failed to meet the mark in math. In contrast, 98 percent of white and Asian students in Princeton High School exceeded grade-level expectations in math and English that same year. In terms of demographics, the school was 47 percent white, 25 percent Asian, 14 percent Latino, and 5 percent Black, with almost 7 percent of students identifying as multiracial. This was not a case of separate and unequal educational facilities. This was all happening in schools that, on paper at least, offered racial diversity within their walls.

A 2005 *New York Times* article about Princeton's difficulties with educating Black children featured a woman named Caroline Mitchell and her seventeen-year-old son, Blake. Caroline had spent the previous few years as president of the high school's alumni association and community liaison for the school district. Her son had graduated the previous year, and by the time he finally walked across the stage, Blake had failed English class in ninth grade and survived a tenth-grade science teacher who said he was a C student who would never get a higher grade. True to her word, though Blake got extra help and tutoring, she never gave him anything more than a C. Despite his mother's protests, her son had spent years in a remedial "basic skills" class. Caroline could not help but notice that, like my child, most of Blake's friends and classmates who struggled at the public school were Black. In April 2006, a local paper detailed how the Princeton police had removed four Black boys from Princeton High School in handcuffs. The night before, a Latino teenager had been beaten, and those who attacked him were Black. No one who witnessed the beating would offer the police information, and a few members of the community had suggested to the police that, given their ages and social connections in the community, it was possible that the Princeton High students might know something about what had happened or be able to assist the police with information about who might have been involved.

The decision to remove these young men from school was made worse by the fact that their parents had already agreed to make the boys voluntarily available to the police after consultation with an attorney. However, the police, citing the need to have the matter resolved and the initial hesitancy of the parents to cooperate, chose instead to show up at the school with police cars and, in front of the whole school, lead the four young men from the building, put them into police cars, and drive them away. As is true in many Black and/or low-income communities, relationships between Princeton's Black community and the police had long been strained, and the show of force and resultant humiliation for the boys became one in a long line of historical incidents, cultural and educational, that buttressed claims of unequal treatment in schools.

Neither Jelani's treatment, nor Blake's, nor that of the young men removed from their school in handcuffs was extraordinary. It is the too-frequent story shared by middle-class and poor Black children alike, both of whom are often routed to and segregated in classrooms that are remedial and majority Black, even within predominantly white districts. And yet, Princeton also had an important role in ending enforced separation and instituting district-wide integration. It was the first district in New Jersey to desegregate its schools, and it did so in a way that became a model for the nation. But before this, Princeton rivaled the South in its commitment to racial and educational segregation.

Most of the historical Black community arrived in the area in the nineteenth century—some as the enslaved property of their southern masters; others hired by the university to serve as butlers, maids, cooks, and chauffeurs. Though not mandated by law as it was in many southern states and towns, racial separation was the expected norm in elementary schools, as well as in the restaurants and stores along Nassau

Street, the main business-lined thoroughfare in town. In 1948, James Baldwin described his racist expulsion from a diner on Nassau Street as the last incident provoking his leaving the United States and taking up permanent residence in France. In his 1958 autobiography, *Here I Stand,* actor, singer, and political activist Paul Robeson wrote that the small town in which he grew up was "spiritually located" in Dixie. "Princeton was Jim Crow," he wrote, before adding, "traditionally the great university—which is practically all there is in town—has drawn a large part of its student body and faculty from below the Mason-Dixon Line, and along with these sons of the bourbons came the most rigid social and economic patterns of White Supremacy."

Before it was integrated, Black children attended the Witherspoon School, and white children went to the Nassau School, about nine blocks away. In the spring of 1948, in response to a lawsuit from the area NAACP arguing that the town was too small to support two separate school systems, and that they were tired of arguing over and for resources, school board members voted to implement what they called the Princeton Plan. It involved school officials combining Black and white students into one school based on grade level, as opposed to trying to figure out how to desegregate the all-white or all-Black schools. District officials began implementing the new policy by placing kindergarteners through fifth graders at the formerly white Nassau School and moving all sixth, seventh, and eighth graders to the formerly all-Black Witherspoon School. Teachers were reassigned to one of the two schools according to their expertise, not based on their race, which served the purpose of integrating the faculties of both schools at the same time as the children were. Without having to contend with the issue of busing white students to undesirable schools, white families in Princeton, unlike the rest of the country, generally viewed integration as having been implemented in a way that was smooth and worry free.

From the first, Princeton's Black residents had some misgivings about the plan to close the segregated Black school. Though this new plan applied to elementary and middle school students, the town's high school had been integrated since 1915, and in a familiar refrain, many Black people felt the white faculty there had ignored or underestimated them and, decades later, their children. "It was a very cold feeling being over at the high school," said Fannie Floyd, who attended Princeton High School in the 1930s. "We enjoyed the Witherspoon School because the Black teachers did push us to do well." Shirley Satterfield, another Black resident who attended the Witherspoon School, said that, as far back as 1950, Black students were automatically tracked into workforce development rather than academic studies at the high school and noted that her mother had to talk the assistant principal into letting her take more rigorous classes to prepare for college. During the whole of her high school career, she never saw a guidance counselor.

Though beloved because of the supportive teaching and administrative staff, the Witherspoon School itself was overcrowded and had suffered from years of deferred maintenance until the NAACP made a push for improvements in 1938. That the NAACP campaigned for improvements, not integration, is unsurprising. Local parents, who did not want their children exposed to disdain and obstruction for trying to integrate formerly white schools, opposed it. Clement Price, the late director of the Rutgers Institute on Ethnicity, Culture, and the Modern Experience at Rutgers-Newark, noted, "Those of us who grew up in the civil rights movement or bore witness to the civil rights movement have forgotten that up until that movement, many Blacks supported their segregation from whites in their town, or whites in the state, with the caveat—better treatment in their segregated world." By the early 1990s, a group comprised of Black, white, and Latino parents and community members organized to address the undereducation and resulting underachievement of non-white students. The top item on their agenda was recruiting more Black teachers who would both support Black students in majority-white schools and improve their lagging achievement levels. They had modest success, but the achievement gap remained, and the district's difficulties with educating Black children continued well into the twenty-first century.

Because of the experiences I had with my son in Princeton public schools, I began to think deeply about racism, segregation, and integration—not just as a parent learning to navigate the reality of integrated school buildings in a wealthy suburban district, but as a scholar and academic. Though to that point my scholarship had focused on Black women in the nineteenth and twentieth centuries, educational inequality began to loom much larger in my academic life. By 2010, I began a multiyear education project that involved a partnership with Trenton public schools, the urban and struggling school district about ten miles south of Princeton. I also began teaching a class at Princeton focused on racism in public education. What I knew by then was Black students in wealthy, integrated districts, like those attending schools that were poor and segregated, struggled to receive the same educations as white students in public schools all over the United States. I hoped I could be part of an effort to bring change and wanted to see if there were any students at Princeton who might want to join me and take a class I designed to explore these issues.

"What's the purpose of education?" one of my students named Ben asked his classmates in the first class I taught on the topic. We were sitting around a table in Stanhope Hall, which was the home of the African American Studies department, where I worked at the time. I was teaching a freshman seminar for students new to college called "Our Struggling Schools: Race, Culture and Urban Education." His classmates tossed back opinions: to teach students to be good citizens. To make money. To get a good job. "There's what we hope the purpose of education is," said another student named Courtney, making the point that in reality, rural and urban schools were plagued by repeated failures and appalling inequalities. What was notable about the exchange is that it took place during a break in the class and, also, that a reporter was present that day to observe us. When the reporter asked why the students had stuck around for a philosophical discussion during the only pause in a three-hour class, Ben said, "We really want to talk about something this important. Our discussion helped me solidify my thoughts." He later said he was working hard to understand how schools and both historical and contemporary efforts to reform urban education were linked to the social, economic, and political conditions of cities. My first assignment for the group of Asian, Black, and white students was to write an essay about how racism, neighborhoods, wealth, and class impacted their educational experiences before arriving at college, a topic they said they had not spent much time previously thinking about. A student named Adeline told the reporter, "Looking at education from a racial perspective has been really interesting," before adding, "We read about *Brown vs. Board of Ed.*, and segregation in schools hasn't changed much since then." I designed the class to ask them to think about the historical and contemporary issues plaguing the educational experiences of many Black children in Princeton, but I had also arranged for the class to participate in a project to assist the superintendent of Trenton public schools by conducting a few experiments aimed at raising low student performance.

As I was new to educational research, I didn't know that it was quite unusual for a professor to just make an appointment with the school superintendent and say, "Hi, I am a professor at Princeton and would like to put together a class to study the problems you would like us to help you solve," but that is exactly what happened, and the work my students did in class became part of a larger initiative focused on urban education reform through providing academic assistance to local school districts. The students in the class all took the opportunity for such real-world engagement to heart and, during the semester, researched tutoring and after-school programs, charter school curriculums, and other innovations in education guided by one simple question: Does it actually work? At the end of the class, we presented our

findings, developed in consultation with classroom teachers, pointing
to the benefit of structured tutoring programs and social and emotional learning programs in raising math and reading test scores to the
superintendent. We were all gratified when we learned the partnership
with the schools in Trenton would extend to another year, this time
incorporating real-world application, with a newly opened school for
grades three through eight as the testing site for our ideas. The school
placed special emphasis on parental involvement and student motiva-
tion to improve student performance. "I wasn't really aware of what
was happening in Trenton" until enrolling in the class, said a student
named Monica, who told the reporter, "I'm interested in how you solve
this problem, and what's keeping others from solving it."

Trenton public schools do not fare well in comparison to Princeton or, for that matter, to most of the schools in New Jersey. Roughly
28 percent of the city's eighty-five thousand residents are poor, almost
twice the state average, and 16 percent live on less than $10,000 a year.
As a result, there is little tax base to support local schools, and the various challenges related to this deficit have defeated almost every educational solution ever tried in the city. Given the lack of wealthy white
people or schools in the district, integration had never been a part of
the educational conversation. In 2010, when we began working with
the district, nearly one-quarter of residents lacked health care, and violent crime was and remains close to the highest in the state.

By 2018, math proficiency among city students, 98 percent of
whom were Black or Latino, remained stubbornly lodged in the single digits, and six of twenty schools in the city earned a score of 10 or
less on the state's 100-point evaluation system. These scores meant the
schools had completely failed. That same year, a Trenton parent named
Yasmeen Douglas said her daughter's second-grade teacher went on
sick leave the second week of September and just never came back.
Yasmeen had no choice but to pull her child from the school. "She
didn't have a teacher the rest of the year until she went into the charter

school in November," Yasmeen recalled. "She didn't have homework the whole year, she didn't even get a progress report before she left." Another parent named Janie Randolph had attended Trenton schools through high school. At the time, her goal was to become an executive assistant. As a student at Trenton Central High School, she said, eleventh-grade social studies had been so basic—such as learning the names of states and their capitals—that though she was a student who consistently earned As and Bs, when arriving at community college, she was immediately placed in two remedial math classes and a remedial English class, because her preparation had been so poor.

When a news crew visited Central High School in Trenton in 2014, the conditions were strikingly like those my students and I observed in 2010. Teachers told the journalists that the building was rotting inside and out, was unhealthy and unsafe, and warned the visitors against drinking the water, which ran from the tap sporting a rich, brown color. In much of the building, the old central ventilation system had been turned off, and the custodians said turning it on might spread asbestos. In one classroom, the reporters noticed that the ceiling was discolored, and the plaster was crumbling. The teacher whose room it was, Mrs. Bridgett Ruggiano, explained the pattern of the stains, distinguishing between leaks from the bathroom above and those caused by rainwater before sharing her bigger concern. In a corner of the room, she pointed to a tiny mousehole and told the reporters, "I can smell the dead mice in the wall." The NBC reporters said they heard similar stories about mold, mildew, falling plaster, water leaks, rodents, and more throughout the building. When I visited the school with my students, we learned that there had once been a college track for students, but that it had been a few years since there had been teachers qualified to prepare them. Instead, the school focused on vocational education, teaching students to become cosmetologists, mechanics, and bus drivers. In 2010, among Black students in Princeton, 64 percent met state expectations on standardized tests. This number is much lower than

the 98 percent of white and Asian students who did so, but still significantly higher than the Black students in Trenton. In 2021–2022,
among New Jersey's 2,105 schools, three of the thirty worst-rated were
in Trenton.

In late April 2011, as we were implementing the project in the new
school, a young woman who was taking part in it came to see me. She
was participating in the structured tutoring program portion of the
study, which the school system could potentially replicate and use to
help raise minority achievement levels. There were forty Princeton students working on the project and two hundred more on a waiting list.
It is worth noting that, despite our best efforts, we were able to get
only four Black students to participate and no Latino students. This is
important because the school we were in was 99.8 percent Black and
Latino. It may also be worth mentioning that all the Black students
were women. In a nutshell, the woman who came to talk with me
wanted me to know that she and some of the other Black women tutors
had noticed that the students responded very differently to them compared to the white tutors—particularly those who were white women.
It wasn't, she was careful to point out, that the students were disre-
spectful toward the Black tutors. But the middle school students were
more *interested* in the lives, backgrounds, and thoughts of the white
tutors. They asked for personal advice, wanted to be mentored by, and
in general were friendlier to and more open in interactions with the
white women tutoring them. The Black tutors wanted advice about
what to do. I didn't really know what to tell them. I knew that confident white students were unusual in the overwhelmingly Black school
and city and, also, that Black faces may have been less of a curiosity
to the overwhelmingly Black students and teachers at the school. Perhaps exposure to the white students was new and exciting for children
not used to seeing people who did not look like them, or perhaps they
had internalized mass-media representations of white people that continued to present them as more impressive and successful than Black

people. It's impossible to know what exactly accounted for the feelings the Black children had and experienced toward the white Princeton students. I do know, though, that segregation harms and distorts in ways we do not always recognize but that matter.

Meanwhile, on Princeton's campus, the topic of education reform was everywhere. Because Wendy Kopp had come up with the idea for what would become Teach for America while a senior at the school, the subject already loomed large, and for many of my students, Kopp occupied rock-star status. But it wasn't just TFA that excited students. Between the 1990s and 2000, various charter school chains, venture capitalist firms, and consulting firms focusing on educational policy and reform and on narrowing the opportunity and achievement gaps between wealthy and impoverished students began to recruit on campus, with success rates that rivaled those of financial services companies. Wealthy titans of industry (often billionaires) began proposing solutions and funding educational "innovations" or experiments. There was even a recently released film, *Waiting for Superman,* that highlighted struggling schools and communities and discussed fixing the system as an extension of the civil rights movement.

Initially, I was totally, and pretty much uncritically, enthusiastic about all of it. It was exciting that so many were interested and involved in improving our flailing educational system. But as time went on, I couldn't help but notice that, like the students who were most involved in participating in the tutoring project, many recruited and interested in these educational innovations were white and came from middle- and upper-middle-class schools. They didn't think it was important to include families and caregivers and students in discussions about what they wanted to see in their neighborhoods, communities, and schools, and much of what was touted as positive interventions involved teaching students in these schools how to raise their hands, sit up straight, take tests, and learn to accept stringent discipline.

While none of these things in and of themselves are necessarily negative, there was a discrepancy between what were considered opportunity leveling educational strategies in working-class and poor communities and what children in high-achieving districts and private schools got. I began to wonder why, to "save" students who were disenfranchised, we had to first teach them to sit, speak, listen, dress, and quietly move through school spaces, disturbing no one. I wondered why the idiosyncratic forms of education on offer to them were worlds apart from the education offered to the wealthy and privileged, who are allowed to sit and stand as they wish. Then I started to notice how interconnected many of the leading figures in this burgeoning urban and rural education reform business were in terms of educational backgrounds, philanthropic support and influences, and friendships. Some students who were part of my program fell in with this thinking. Soon our partnership with Trenton schools fell apart.

Overall, during our yearlong engagement with the district, we found that individualized and structured tutoring programs that served as a continuation of daily classroom lessons worked much better than did programs primarily focused on students getting well-meaning help with their homework. We also learned that social and emotional learning activities that helped students identify and name big feelings, like the difference between being tired and angry, and gave them tools for responding appropriately for the emotion were more impactful than tutoring in improving educational outcomes. We learned that children having a secure place to live, stable and present caretakers, and enough food to feel content also mattered. In many ways, what those few years taught me was that a broken safety net leads to a broken educational system, which, at worst, breaks children and, at best, consigns them to the lower rungs of the social and economic ladder. Poverty exacerbates the problems involved in Black education but isn't the whole story. Our partnership with the city of Trenton ended after it came to light that many white Princeton students had begun to refer to the Black students they were there to tutor and train in derogatory ways, believing them to be wild "jungle dwellers," and sharing within earshot of the Black tutors and program participants that teaching the poor Black students was a waste of time, because they were unable to learn—thinking that echoed the eugenicist ideas planted in the 1970s. Segregation leads white people to hold and perpetuate negative views of Black people. No one is well served by it.

My multiyear partnership left me with more questions than answers. Of course, back in Princeton, my own child's surroundings and economic opportunities could not have been more different. The violence he experienced wasn't the violence of poverty; it was something else equally devastating. Jelani's childhood offered him a seeming level of comfort, if not the possibility for unqualified acceptance into our overwhelmingly white and affluent community. His father and I were able to breathe just a bit more easily knowing that there were ways in which where we lived kept certain types of social instability at bay, even as we knew his seeming intimate acceptance into the homes and lives of his white friends would not shield him from the reality of racial stereotypes, invective, or eventual trauma. We knew that poor, working-class, or urban communities were not the only places where Black boys are terrorized and traumatized. We knew that the unfamiliarity of his white friends with any other Black people would one day become an issue in our home. We knew that guns were not the only way to murder a soul.

For those reasons, as the moments first arrived, then intensified, we were not surprised. But we were overwhelmed by and unprepared for how often white adults, school officials, and parents worked in seeming unison to turn every act of racial aggression aimed at our son into an opportunity to explain how he was responsible for the behavior of his white friends and classmates. He, we were told, wrung the racism from the mouths, souls, and bodies of his white teammates, classmates, and acquaintances. If he would just try harder to fit in a little better, we were told by parents and adults, these clashes would not occur.

The first time we heard this, Jelani was thirteen. One of his school-mates at the private school where we had been forced to send him called him a nigger at the end of a softball game that their team lost. In the verbal sparring that followed the game, Jelani said something that made the other boys laugh at the child who had started the argument. In response, as the boys turned their laughter on him, this young man who was Jelani's friend said, "Well, at least I'm not a nigger." Jelani stopped laughing. The boy turned red. He pushed Jelani. Jelani pushed back. An adult arrived to break up the crowd and told both the boys to come to school the next day with their parents. Bill and I arrived at the school expecting an apology. Surely, the verbal violence this child had hurled warranted that, we thought. Instead, we were told the boys owed each other apologies. Their "logic" was that Jelani was also in the wrong because had he not made others laugh at the racial epithet–hurling child, nothing unpleasant would have happened. One of the boy's parents said their child probably learned that word from Jelani in the first place because, the parents assured the school principal, no one in their house talked like that. Of course, by the time the meeting was over, we were all clear that Jelani apologizing to someone who had both called him a nigger and then pushed him first was not something that would be taking place. Nonetheless, a version of this same scenario of inverted responsibility happened so often that, as time passed, we grew less and less surprised.

The second incident took place a few months later. Jelani was in a science lab, and the students were told to pair up to complete a series of experiments. Jelani, who was popular with his peers and valued for his athletic skills and his humor, already had a partner. A different young man in the class demanded that Jelani get rid of his first partner and pair up with him instead. When Jelani refused, the scorned partner took a ballpoint pen and rammed it into Jelani's thigh. The pen pierced the skin. Drops of blood formed around the wound. The pen clung to my son's thigh, he told us, seemingly as if floating in midair. During the meeting following that attack, the same school principal told us that Jelani would have to learn that, while in his home "community" treating others poorly might be acceptable, at this school he had to treat his classmates with respect. Jelani had apparently hurt this young man's feelings when he declined to pair up with him, and since the unchosen partner had a history of emotional problems, clearly no one should think to hold him responsible. Again, there would be no apology.

The last time I know about that Jelani was submitted to or a witness to racial violence from a "friend" was when he was a senior in high school playing soccer for his club team. One of his teammates screamed, "Stop that nigger!" from the sidelines, pointing his teammates on the field to the opposing team's star player. When Jelani took offense, the coach, who had known him since he was ten, told him he was overreacting, to "calm down." My son's "friend" who did the hollering said, "But I wasn't talking about you. I don't think of you that way." It's worth noting that research on racial perception proves that having diverse friends doesn't make one immune to race-based prejudice, whether conscious or not. That explains why that teammate's characterization of my son did not extend to the unknown Black player on the field. This is a far too frequent experience for children who desegregate predominantly white schools. What I remember most about Jelani and his educational journey in Princeton is not so much the university for which the town was named, the pretty shops, graceful houses, or the liberal city government. Other than the sky-high taxes, what I most remember is how often my son was racially harassed, disrespected, and aggressed by his white friends and their parents. I remember how rare it was for his friends or teachers to protect him. I remember how, once finally wrestled, the apologies were perfunctory. I remember the insistence, aggressively uttered and believed, that the various perpetrators were "good children" from "good families." I remember how fully we as a family came to understand that schools were places of great opportunity and, at the same time, that Black children required layers of protection to survive them whole.

The American education system is a tale of two universes. Whenever you hear that America has fallen behind and is at the bottom of various world rankings, what that really means is that districts like Trenton, which are (either rural or urban) poor and overwhelmingly of color, are pulling down the rest of the system. The educational debate in this country is centered on how to "fix" this drag on the overall system. But few ever want to talk about race in this debate, except to say that it is racist to think that Black children can't learn. Since the 1980s and the end of policy initiatives to aid in desegregation, our educational discussions have become devoid of historical context, as if these underperforming school districts have come to exist in a vacuum and not as a direct result of seventy years of violence, underfunding, over policing, hostility, and neglect—largely if not primarily because of white racism. Meanwhile, we have moved further and further way from the original goal of *Brown* and its proponents: to better and more fairly educate *all* Black children. We are at a point when we might ask if we are coroners or surgeons. Is our goal when we say we want to fix public education to bury or heal the educational body politic?

COLLEGE ACCESS
AND COMMUNITY SCHOOLS

In the 1940s, Swedish Nobel laureate economist Gunnar Myrdal was enlisted by the Carnegie Foundation to lead a study on the obstacles to full civic and societal inclusion of Black people in the United States. The foundation believed that, as a non-American, Myrdal could offer a more unbiased opinion than an American would. No one thought to ask a Black person to author the report, but Ralph Bunche, a Black political scientist and diplomat who won the 1950 Nobel Peace Prize for his work in the Middle East, consulted on the project, contributing over three thousand pages of research. The resulting report, *An American Dilemma: The Negro Problem and Modern Democracy,* clocked in at nearly 1,500 pages and reflected Myrdal's conclusion that racism and the disparate treatment of white and Black people could be resolved if white Americans merely became aware that it existed.

According to Myrdal, southern white people needed the benefit of the knowledge and expertise of their northern neighbors—who he assumed were unaware of the racial segregation and Jim Crow oppression present in the South—to learn to be less racist. If northern white people were made aware, and southerners learned from their northern neighbors, he believed, racism in the United States would fade. He was naive. It never occurred to Myrdal that white people, institutions, and educational systems in the North were as committed to racial segregation, especially in schools, as anywhere else. Bunche, on the other hand, was doubtful that white people had much reason to feel angst about or feel inspired to change a system that, organized around ideas of Black inferiority and white superiority, benefited them.

The vast distance between their views was illustrated by their responses to a visit they made to a southern jail. While there, Myrdal ate lunch with the warden while Bunche was forced to eat with the Black chain gang—prisoners who worked outside doing hard labor while chained together at the ankle. Later, when the two discussed their treatment, Myrdal thought the difference in their treatment was because the sheriff had not known that this distinction existed. This, he thought, was evidence of the "American dilemma." Once the injustice of this situation was made known to the warden, Myrdal believed he would feel guilt, which would motivate him to act. Bunche, however, doubted that the warden was ignorant of racial oppression or separation in the South, or even in his jail. The pair had very different worldviews about what was required to bring about racial equity.

Still, once published, Myrdal's *An American Dilemma* was a literary event. It sold over one hundred thousand copies, went through twenty-five printings, and was enormously influential in shaping the ways policymakers, philanthropists, and politicians viewed racism in the United States, even as Bunche believed Myrdal's conclusions to be unsophisticated, wrongheaded, and lacking in accurate racial analysis. This book, cited in the *Brown v. Board* case, was generally positive in its outlook on the future of "race relations," believing that segregation in housing and education would soon end as southern whites learned to think more like their northern neighbors.

Of course, this did not happen. To this day, educational segregation is alive and well both inside and outside the South, and all that followed the *Brown* decision is proof that educational change will require more than either a change of heart or a court order. In our present, up to 90 percent of the schools in major metropolitan areas like Chicago, New York, Philadelphia, Los Angeles, and Dallas are heavily racially segregated. A report called *Racial Segregation Continues, and Even Intensifies* by the Economic Policy Institute argues that the exposure of the average Black student to white people is less today than it was in 1940 and has remained mostly unchanged since 1950. The impacts of school segregation extend beyond the classroom. For example, Black, Latino, and Asian Americans who live in areas with high percentages of racially segregated schools face higher medical costs. According to a 2022 study in *Pediatrics,* the journal for the American Academy of Pediatrics, eliminating these types of inequities would have reduced medical care expenditures paid by the federal government by nearly $230 billion. That is money that could have been used to equally fund public school districts, like those in Detroit or Trenton. On top of this, more than a trillion additional dollars in lost wages and reduced productivity were associated with health inequities directly related to students who attend highly segregated schools. I mention these sums in the hope that perhaps if they are large enough, it might finally seem worthwhile for lawmakers and politicians to agree to equally fund, educate, and support the schools that Black children attend. Racial residential and educational segregation even in the primary grades can have long-lasting effects, negatively impacting if and where students go to college and what type of university they attend. This is our true and continuing American dilemma, affecting health, democracy, and college attainment.

A few years ago, a report looking at racial segregation in the Gifted and Talented program in New York City makes the consequences for such levels of segregation in education clear. The authors found that "accelerated classrooms serve as pipelines to the city's highest-achievement middle schools and high schools, creating a cycle in which students who start out ahead get even further advantages from the city's schools." And a book called *Taming the River,* authored by sociologists at the University of Pennsylvania, found that when looking at achievement data for Black and Latino students in the top thirty high schools in the country, two-thirds of the difference between their scores and grades and those of their white and Asian peers could be predicted based on the degree of racial segregation in the neighborhoods and schools from which Black students came. These levels of racial separation continue to allow intolerance to grow and makes change more difficult.

Given the state of K–12 schools that educate most Black people, it shouldn't surprise us that Black college and university enrollment has been dropping steadily over the past twenty-five years. Black student college enrollment began to drop steadily in the 1980s and dropped further between 2010 and 2020, representing more than 650,000 students who, according to the National Center for Education Statistics, skipped out on college. Following the pandemic, the numbers have continued to fall, according to figures from the National Student Clearinghouse Research Center. Forty-five percent of Black children attend majority-Black, majority-poor schools, compared with 8 percent of white students who attend under-resourced schools. According to a 2018 analysis of federal data by the Center for American Progress, based on a survey of twenty-three thousand students who started ninth grade in 2009, even the highest-achieving low-income students went to college at lower rates than their more affluent counterparts. The wealthiest students with mediocre academic backgrounds were just as likely to enroll as the lowest-income students with the highest grades and test scores. "It's tempting to think that America has largely solved its problems surrounding access to postsecondary education," the Center for American Progress report said. In fact, it said, the data shows "the United States still fails miserably" at educating Black children.

Even those who do enroll in a college or university risk making choices that sink them deeper into a cycle of inequality. The issue of where a Black student obtains their college degree is important, because all college degrees are not created equal. If students' intentions in obtaining a college degree are to change their economic trajectory, build wealth for themselves and future generations, better insulate themselves and their families from economic upheaval and recession, and contribute to the tax base of their towns, cities, and the nation, then they would do well to avoid both for-profit institutions and two-year colleges and to opt instead for degrees from four-year institutions. But many Black students lack the relevant information about what kinds of degrees matter, so their decisions may exacerbate the social and economic inequalities a college degree is meant to ameliorate.

While it is hard to argue that the pursuit and attainment of college degrees are anything but good news, as we all prepare ourselves for the end of affirmative action in higher education, general statistics about college enrollment and completion for Black students bear some warnings. Of students who graduate from for-profit programs, 98 percent do so with crushing debt, struggle to find employment up to a year after graduation and earn lower salaries than students who graduate from four-year institutions. That disparity is also troublesome for students who graduate with two-year degrees. In addition to the rapid increase in Black student enrollment at for-profit colleges, it is important to keep in mind that in California, for example, almost 70 percent of Black students who attend college at all are in two-year institutions. What all this means is that, taken together, community colleges and for-profit colleges account for over 60 percent of Black student enrollment in college. Our current K–12 system of education is not helping Black students achieve but is instead continually pulling them backward and down.

There is one hopeful development taking place that threads the needle between individuals changing their hearts and institutions changing their ways. It is worth noting that this development is also a powerful way to educate Black children well and make sure they are well taken care of in classrooms near their homes and communities regardless of demographics. The solution, community schools, offers separate but equal—if not superior—institutions, and the model is spreading quickly. Community schools are based on the Black Panther Party's educational concept and reflect what's possible in neighborhoods where there were few to no white people with whom to integrate. It is focused on providing Black and Latino children with a quality educational experience in the public school system.

The school opened by the Black Panthers in 1973 was based on the pioneering idea that a school should be designed to address community needs and care for the "whole child." Oakland Community School was located in East Oakland, where some of the city's most vulnerable children lived, and was one of the first schools to provide basic and holistic support for its low-income students, such as providing three meals a day, teaching them to express and manage their feelings using meditation or yoga, and providing access to free medical care at the community health clinics opened by the Panthers. The first children who sat down to a free breakfast before school ate chocolate milk, eggs, bacon, sausage, cereal, and fresh oranges. The federal government had not at that point begun providing free breakfast for economically vulnerable children, so this simple, and today completely unremarkable, occurrence was notable. In 2010, three decades after the Black Panthers' community school experiment wound down in 1981, the Oakland Unified School District revived the idea for all K–12 grades. These new schools, also called community schools, are in effect a twenty-first-century version of separate but equal schools that, with few exceptions, were not often allowed to exist.

Since 2010, Oakland's district-wide transformation of its schools to the new community school model has served as an example for positive educational reform. The results are impressive so far. Dropout rates fell from 25 percent to 13 percent between the 2011–12 and 2020–21 school years, and the number of students reading at or above grade level rose from 22 percent in 2011 to 37 percent in the 2017–18 school year. In 2024, sixty-one schools across the state of California will receive five-year state grants to aid them in transitioning to the community school model. Curtiss Sarikey, the Oakland Unified School District chief of staff who leads the community school expansion effort, said, "The reason that community schools have not just grown but actually thrived—over five superintendents, over a decade, over strikes, over Covid, over school closures—is because there was so much bottom-up buy-in from the get-go." Unlike what took place leading up to the construction and opening of Potrero Hill Middle School, the planning for these schools promotes democracy, civic engagement, and community input and buy-in from the beginning.

Given the success in Oakland, in 2022 the state awarded San Francisco Unified School District $34 million, and hundreds of schools across California received $4 billion to undergo the same transition. Though California has stepped up in funding community schools, the fact that the entire effort depends on temporary funding could impede their ability to make a lasting impact. Just as the Black Panthers' earlier effort endured for less than a decade, today's educational experiment might not last either. "They always have an end date," Linda Villarreal, who cowrote a book called *Community Schools Revolution,* said about state grants. "Until community schools are part and parcel of the annual budget, they will struggle for sustainability." Still, while they are with us, community schools show promise to address the consistent undereducation of Black children.

With funding originating at the state level, as well as the incorporation of community input, shared governance, and a variety of social service programs, these types of schools are just what the civil rights attorney David Sciarra sees as a positive intervention. The report he authored, *Equity and Diversity: Defining the Right to Education for the 21st Century,* says that community schools, not failed desegregation strategies, are the balm for the wound that is the United States' legacy of denying Black people educational opportunity. The education system defined as unequal by the Supreme Court continues for many of our students, yet educational justice remains elusive. Reversing the decades of racial, economic, and residential segregation that was cemented post-*Brown* and the civil rights era is, at this point, a monumental feat, but in the meantime, community schools present an opportunity to offer Black children targeted, relevant support that could help lift them out of the educational wasteland where they've been abandoned. And thanks to recent investments at both the federal and state level, Sciarra notes that thousands of public schools are transforming into hubs that facilitate community-wide collaboration on collective challenges by embracing a "community school" framework.

In 2018, basketball superstar LeBron James opened his own community school in his hometown of Akron, Ohio. A joint effort between Akron Public Schools and the LeBron James Family Foundation, the I Promise School is overseen and operated by the district with additional funding from the foundation. This support means the school can offer students a host of resources that most district schools do not: tuition to the University of Akron after graduation; family services like GED classes and job placement assistance; and housing for students and their parents. During the school's inaugural year, it began with 240 students in third and fourth grade. Students, who must already attend a public school in Akron and fall into the bottom 30th percentile of reading scores to be admitted, are selected via lottery. The school website says that it is dedicated "to those students who are already falling behind and in danger of falling through the cracks." It aims to "move students forward at a rate of one and a third years' worth of growth in one year," which would "get a student who is two years behind in third grade back on track before they reach high school."

The students at the school, much like those whom earlier generations of Black people opened private schools to educate, were identified as the worst performers in the Akron public schools and branded with behavioral problems. These were not cherry-picked, high-performing students. Some as young as eight were considered at risk of not even graduating from elementary school. Sixty percent of the students who attend I Promise are Black, 15 percent speak another primary language other than English, and almost 30 percent are listed as "special education" students. In addition, a majority are overwhelmingly poor, with three-quarters qualifying as low-income. The school has a $2 million budget that is funded by the district. This is the same basic amount per pupil that the district spends in other schools, but James's foundation provides about $600,000 per year for additional teaching staff to help reduce class sizes and provide an additional hour of after-school programming and tutors.

During the first few years it was open, according to an analysis of the school conducted by the Fordham Institute, the results seemed to suggest there really was such a thing as a silver bullet. In April 2019, the school announced on Twitter that "90 percent of its students had met or exceeded their expected growth in math and reading" on a national test that measures growth over the course of a year. The school only earned a C on statewide assessments, a score that would typically be distressingly low for middle-class schools, but for a school full of vulnerable children, the fact that it was meeting basic expectations with students who had started a year or two behind grade level was good news. If that kind of growth had continued, the school would be well on its way to becoming a model for how to educate similar children around the country.

But then the pandemic hit, and as was true for schools all over the country, math and reading test scores plummeted. School closures, remote learning, and a plethora of other issues combined to produce whopping learning losses nationwide, most especially among students who were Black, poor, and the most vulnerable—the very same students the new school sought to serve and who were already years behind their peers before the pandemic hit. On top of all the existing issues that regularly left communities, students, families, and students reeling, this was just one more hurdle too tall to hop over. As a nation, we have dug a hole for ourselves that is daunting to contemplate filling.

Despite the regression caused by the pandemic, there is reason to maintain our faith in community schools. In a sense, these institutions are an attempt to reembrace the idea of schools as social, political, and communal places, while also compensating for the compounding effects of racism by offering mental health and social services, meals, tutoring, and after-school programs, among other resources. The choice of which services each school needs is made collectively by students, parents, and staff. "The school is in the community, and the community is in the school," wrote Villarreal in *Community School Revolution*. This approach is based on the idea that when schools provide support to the whole child and their families and build strong partnerships with community organizations and businesses, becoming more firmly embedded in communities, student learning outcomes will improve, particularly in under-resourced, marginalized communities.

This type of multifaceted strategy is necessary because, as a 2011 study on Chicago schools concluded, piecemeal strategies—like busing or school investment alone—are insufficient for improving children's education in poor neighborhoods. These types of communities had high crime rates and inadequate community supports (such as health care and social service providers). The students moved frequently and had low-income parents with relatively little formal education and a high likelihood of unemployment. The investigators concluded, "Our findings about schooling in truly disadvantaged communities offer a sobering antidote to a heady political rhetoric arguing that all schools can be improved." A variety of research studies emphasize the optimistic results among schools serving Black children that had well-developed curriculums, offered collaboration between teachers and principals, and made a concerted effort to involve parents and the community. Students where this approach is implemented make substantially greater academic progress compared to those in schools without these characteristics. But the University of Chicago–based research team discovered that even these interventions made little difference in schools serving neighborhoods of concentrated poverty, often majority Black. These are just the types of neighborhoods and children most in need of impactful, well-rounded schools and caring teachers.

Yet today, there remains continued resistance to making the sorts of investments and changes required to repair our broken public education system. According to public opinion polls, like the one commissioned in 2017 in a collaboration between NPR, the Robert Wood Johnson Foundation, and the Harvard T.H. Chan School of Public Health, when asked about racial justice and equality today, majorities believe that we as a nation have done everything reasonable to end racial oppression and inequality, and some even think that civil rights policies may have gone so far as to be unfair to white people. Many, including the Georgetown University scholar Richard Kahlenberg, believe that affirmative action efforts should center on class rather than racial backgrounds. And with the Supreme Court's summer 2023 decision to ban race-based affirmative action policies, we now must all accept the color-blind view of the current Supreme Court majority, which supports the idea that both educational segregation and racial tolerance reflect individual choices rather than state or government action. None of this is accurate. State legislatures, the federal government, and individual white parents have deliberately created a system in which educational segregation benefits the wealthy and the privileged and inflicts harm on almost everyone else. And we should be doing more, not less, to help bridge that gap.

The "Massive Resistance" to integration and equitable educations for Black children continues almost completely unabated, with neither the national will, nor any consistently applied plan, to change it. Instead of focusing on what we know works—small classes, high-quality teachers, adequate funding, and wrap-around social services—in the last thirty years, government, philanthropy, business, and financial sectors have heavily invested in efforts to privatize certain segments of public education, such as providing vouchers to wealthy parents to use to send their children to private or religious schools, or expanding privately run, publicly funded charter schools. But the solution is neither adherence to failed desegregation strategies nor idiosyncratic forms of education that benefit everyone but Black children. At this point, we can either continue to encourage chaos by allowing our tax dollars to be used to experiment educationally on working-class and poor children and disrupt poor communities by closing schools, or we can finally and once and for all deliver on our promise of educating all Black children in the same way that we do the wealthy and the white. The choices we make will tell future generations much of what they will need to know about what our democracy means to us in the twenty-first century. We have time to make change, but as always, the question is, do we have the will to either force white parents to comply with desegregation and integration strategies or to fully embrace a system that is, like Gibbs Junior College in 1960s Pinellas County, Florida, separate and truly equal?

If communities allow it, integration works—on a social and educational level. But to achieve it, we need collective buy-in. White, wealthy schools, neighborhoods, and parents would need to truly embrace integration strategies and be intentional about racial and ethnic inclusion. Negative perceptions and attitudes toward Black children would need to be tackled so their schools do not become hostile spaces. The compounding effects of racism and residential segregation would need to be addressed and remedied to ensure Black children's paths are cleared. Black teachers would need to be hired to anchor students who are often misunderstood or neglected. It would be a massive and worthwhile undertaking. But history does not make me optimistic about our collective will to do what needs to be done. Community schools are the next-best option—or at the very least, a solid first step.

Perhaps, once we tackle the urgent needs of the segregated schools in which many Black children have been languishing, we might be able to move toward and gain support for integration strategies like reciprocal busing. The community school model meets us where we are and sets us on a path toward equity.

Having spent almost two decades studying the intersections of how the past and present of segregation, economics, and educational policies intertwine and encircle schools, textbooks, teachers, and students, I know that education is politics by other means—one of the many issues picked up and dropped by politicians at their convenience. I do not believe we can continue to ignore the soul-shattering experiences of children and young adults, the pain in the voices of grassroots activists and family caregivers, or the incredulous stories told by journalists who cover the aftermath of integration, segregation, and desegregation disasters. The continuation of structural racism in the United States concentrates Black students in public schools that have fewer resources, lower per-student expenditures, fewer AP courses, and teachers who are less experienced than those in suburban schools. And the disparity in resources available to majority-Black schools compared to wealthier schools leads to measurable differences in the quality of Black students' educational experiences, ensuring, among other disadvantages, that fewer are sufficiently prepared to win the race that is the competitive college-admissions process.

Black teachers pre-*Brown* fought hard for a world in which their students did not just work and learn, but where they and their children could also live, breathe, and be. Schools and teachers have never just been about imparting knowledge from books. Like the Black church, schools served as spaces where leaders gathered to plan community protests and legal challenges to resist the efforts of elected and unelected white supremacists to deny Black people the franchise. The destruction of the Black education infrastructure shook one of the pillars upholding Black politics and activism. The more I have learned about my grandparents and their friends, the more I have come to believe it was white supremacy, wrapped in the soft glove of integration, that caused my grandfather's heart attack and my grandmother to live the last decades of her life in an increasingly suffocating isolation. It certainly caused the trauma suffered by both Black teachers and students in the aftermath of *Brown,* when the rage-filled backlash to the decision was as swift as it was devastating. Too few of us have a memory of segregated Black schools as the beating heart of vibrant Black communities, enabling students to compose lives of harmony, melody, and rhythm and sustained Black life and dignity.

One starting point for why I wrote this book was the day I read an article about how city officials in Clearwater had decided to build a school on land that held the bodies of Black people. I couldn't get out of my head that the land beneath my feet had once cradled our community's dead. This defilement seemed an apt metaphor for how often Black progress comes at the expense of Black history, heritage, and legacy. Raised as I was by parents and grandparents who not only valued education but knew how to grieve the dead, I decided to tell a story inspired by the broken chalkboards and dreams of integration. It is a Black story, an American story, a human story, and a national history. As you, reader, know by now, these integration stories include those of my grandparents, southern Black teachers who fought hard with books, organizing tactics, and even guns for integration to come, not knowing before it was too late that it would hasten the disintegration of the Black community they had lovingly fostered. That of my father, a valedictorian, a dean's list student, and also, according to professors and peers at the law school at UC Berkeley, a slacker who was bound to fail. Over time, the lack of support and community led to him losing a long-fought battle to keep drug and alcohol abuse at bay. My own story, which involves integrated classrooms in which I learned a variety of survival strategies, including the truth that, along with mastering my academic work, my personal work involved understanding how to hide racial truths, perspectives, ways of sounding and being Black that would make my white teachers and classmates uncomfortable. And finally, my son's story: that of a star athlete and academically gifted student in academically competitive, overwhelmingly white schools and classrooms who nonetheless had to navigate a world where teachers didn't believe he could read as well as he did, write as well as he does, and had to prove again and again that he belonged, that he "deserved" to be among his peers.

The paradox here is that ours is, by most measures, an educational trajectory that should prove convincingly that the battle to integrate schools in the United States was one worth fighting. I have taught at a variety of Ivy League universities. My son attended one of the top-ranked liberal arts colleges in the nation, Amherst, and is firmly ensconced in a company at the top of the Fortune 500 list. We have realized dreams my grandparents could have scarcely imagined. We are part of the minority whom desegregation helped propel into coveted positions typically inaccessible to people who look like us. We integrated. But at the same time, thinking about those children left behind in schools that meant them no good, in the care of teachers who meant them harm reminded me again and again of bodies forgotten on land that was desecrated. Unable to shake the image and to excise the ghosts in any other way, I wrote a book about what and whom integration left behind as a way of determining what might be worth rescuing from the rubble of our collective past in the hopes of finding a way to bridge the continuing racial divides in the United States.

The complete story of education in the United States is operatic in its dramatic highs and overwrought lows. The peaks and valleys rise and fall in three distinct registers that sometimes harmonize, and sometimes diverge into discord. The higher register is a song of white skin and life-altering access to power and privilege. The lower register is the reality of too little money invested in the people, schools, neighborhoods, and communities where Black, brown, and poor children live.

It is a story of citizenship distorted and the sticky reality of caste from which learning alone cannot free children. The third register wraps itself around the other two. It is the sometimes transformative, sometimes emotionally devastating tune of many Black, brown, and poor children who desegregate predominantly white and wealthy schools. Educational sociologist Gloria Ladson-Billings says that, for Black people, the aftermath of how integration policies were implemented is akin to "landing on the wrong note," as happens when, during a performance, a musician's finger lands on a note that brings discord instead of an integrated harmony. When I first read that, my mind conjured hands moving across the length of a piano's keyboard, ignoring the ebony keys to weave segregated harmonies from ivory alone, until a finger loses its way, touches a black key, and changes the sound so completely that it unsettles instead of soothes. The hands resume playing, moving, striking, but avoiding the black keys altogether, taking more care to avoid the black keys at all costs going forward. The results of this strategy are tragic. We should find another way.

ACKNOWLEDGMENTS

In 1802, a heavily pregnant enslaved Black woman named Solitude shouted, "Live free or die" as white men slit her stomach, removed her son, and then executed her for her involvement in a rebellion of the enslaved in Guadeloupe. As she died, her murderers whispered that though she had taken up arms and murdered to ensure her child would be born free, her baby, whom she would never see or hold, would live, but would forever be property. I thought often of Solitude while writing this book about love, sacrifice, hope, ruin, and generational inheritance. I think often of her son and sometimes believe that like a character in a fictional book full of wizards, witches, and magic, maybe his mother's resolve was a protective inheritance that kept him safe as he grew alone.

This is an odd place, I know, to begin these acknowledgments, since neither Solitude nor her motherless son are in this book. But this story, her resolve, his life have haunted me and kept me writing and thinking about love, sacrifice, fight, and survival. They haunt every page. I want them to know that. I want you to know that.

· · ·

I want to thank my agent, Tanya McKinnon, for her unwavering belief that this book had merit and would find an audience, and that I have merit and will find an audience. . . . You are one of one. Thank you!

I want to thank Lisa Lucas, who believed this book should have a home at Pantheon and always made me feel welcomed, seen, and wanted. Thank you!

I want to thank my editor, Concepción de Leon, for her patience, guidance, skill, and willingness. By the end of this process, she was able to match my writing style, rhythm, and word choices with stunning accuracy. She made my writing better in every way. Thank you!

For my son, Jelani, who is my heart, has a beautiful soul, and is one of my biggest cheerleaders. Thank you!

For Bill, my husband and partner in crimes of the mind. I still flutter when you call me your "thirty-mile-woman." Almost thirty years, and I'm regularly grateful. Thank you!

NOTES

INTRODUCTION

4 **using her skin to make the point:** Private conversation between Noliwe Rooks and Public Counsel lawyers Mark Rosenbaum and Amanda Savage, April 10, 2021.

6 **"economic lifelines and community centers":** Adam Fairclough, "The Costs of Brown: Black Teachers and School Integration," *Journal of American History* 91, no. 1 (2004): 43–55.

7 **working well for them:** Charise Chaney, "The Brown v. Board of Education case didn't start how you think it did," *The Conversation,* May 16, 2019, https:// theconversation.com/the-brown-v-board-of-education-case-didnt-start-how -you-think-it-did-117299.

8 **Neither teachers who attempted:** Charles M. Payne, "'The Whole United States Is Southern!': Brown v. Board and the Mystification of Race," *Journal of American History* 91 no. 1 (2004): 83–91.

8 **beating, bombing, and terrorizing:** Campbell F. Scribner, "Surveying the Destruction of African American Schoolhouses in the South, 1864–1876," *Journal of the Civil War Era* 10, no. 4, (2020): 469–94, https://www.jstor.org/stable /26977402. See also, Mark Lieberman, "Racist Bomb Threats and Post-Civil War School Burnings: A Scholar Connects the Dots," *Education Week* (2022): 11.

8   **defecated atop the students' desks:** W. E. B. Du Bois, *The Negro Common School,* no. 6 (Atlanta: Atlanta University Publications, 1901): 38.

9   **"If there are not adequate Negro schools":** Olivia Marcucci, "Zora Neale Hurston and the Brown Debate: Race, Class, and the Progressive Empire," *Journal of Negro Education* 86, no. 1 (2017): 13–24.

11   **"permanent underclass":** Laurence Tribe, "Detroit Denying Kids Equal Opportunity to Succeed," *Boston Herald,* September 30, 2016.

11   **segregated by race and income:** Noliwe Rooks, *Cutting School: Privatization, Segregation, and the End of Public Education* (New York: New Press, 2017), 5.

12   **White resistance was aided by judges:** Ian Miller, " 'Brown v. Board of Education' Didn't End Segregation, Big Government Did," *The Nation,* May 24, 2014, https://www.thenation.com/article/brown-v-board-education-didnt-end -segregation-big-government-did/.

13   **"Negro's blood is on their hands":** NAACP, *Mississippi Is for Murder,* November 1955, 2, https://usm.access.preservica.com/uncategorized/IO_d7161caf -caac-4d51-92d0-7b97effc5533/.

13   **able to stick it out:** Adam Harris, "The Undoing of a Tennessee Town," *The Atlantic,* September 29, 2020, https://www.theatlantic.com/education/archive /2020/09/firsts-undoing-small-tennessee-town/616453/.

16   **"Harry, I want me a boy":** Richard Kluger, *Simple Justice: The History of Brown v. Board of Education and Black America's Struggle for Equality* (New York: Vintage Books, 1977), 25.

16   **arrested the cow:** Kluger, 22.

17   **only southern schools were required to:** Ibid., Miller.

18   **aimed at lessening racism in public policy:** Mark J. Chin, "The impact of school desegregation on White individuals' racial attitudes and politics in adulthood," EdWorkingPaper No. 20-318, 2022, https://doi.org/10.26300/0gag-kf60.

18   **wrong, inequitable, and unjust:** Southern Education, "New Polling Data Finds Widespread Support for Integrating and Fairly Funding Public Schools," 2023, https://southerneducation.org/in-the-news/new-polling-data-finds-widespread -support-for-integrating-and-fairly-funding-public-schools/.

18   **solutions that *require* white parents to comply:** E. Torres and R. Weissbourd, "Do Parents Really Want School Integration?" 2020, https://mcc.gse.harvard .edu/. See also Emma Garcia, "Schools Are Still Segregated, and Black Children

Are Paying a Price," Economic Policy Institute, February 12, 2020, https://www
.epi.org/publication/schools-are-still-segregated-and-black-children-are-paying
-a-price/.

18 **rather be sick than swallow the dose:** Jason Breslow et al., "The Return of
School Segregation in Eight Charts," *Frontline,* July 15, 2014, https://www.pbs
.org/wgbh/frontline/article/the-return-of-school-segregation-in-eight-charts/.

CHAPTER 1: "IT IS THROUGH OUR CHILDREN WE WILL BE FREE."

30 **"downstream consequences":** Jonathan M. Metzl and Dorothy E. Roberts,
"Structural Competency Meets Structural Racism: Race, Politics, and the
Structure of Medical Knowledge." *AMA Journal of Ethics* 16, no. 9 (2014):
682, https://journalofethics.ama-assn.org/article/structural-competency-meets
-structural-racism-race-politics-and-structure-medical-knowledge/2014-09.

30 **"is less overt, far more subtle":** Jonathan M. Metzl and Dorothy E. Roberts,
"Virtual Mentor," *American Medical Association Journal of Ethics* 16, no. 9 (September 2014): 674.

31 **"Structural racism is a public health crisis":** Kesha Moore, "Structural Racism
is a Public Health Crisis," *Thurgood Marshall Institute,* May 20, 2020, https://
tminstituteldf.org/wp-content/uploads/2020/05/Structural-Racism-is-a
-Public-Health-v2.pdf.

31 **long-term exposure to noise:** Peris Eulalia, "Environmental Noise in Europe-
20," *European Environment Agency,* March 5, 2020, https://www.eea.europa.eu
/publications/environmental-noise-in-europe.

32 **they have limited worth:** Cory Turner, "Court Rules Detroit Students Have
Constitutional Right to An Education," NPR, April 27, 2020, https://www.npr
.org/2020/04/27/845595380/court-rules-detroit-students-have-constitutional
-right-to-an-education.

32 **internalized the racism:** Metzl and Roberts.

33 **"prejudice, discrimination, and segregation":** "A Revealing Experiment,"
NAACP Legal Defense Fund, https://www.naacpldf.org/brown-vs-board
/significance-doll-test/.

34 **"I don't feel anymore":** *Gary B. v. Whitmer,* https://www.opn.ca6.uscourts.gov
/opinions.pdf/20a0124p-06.pdf.

34 **"they get to choose our education":** Sara Rosenbaum, *Lies Closed This School* (2019), unreleased film on literacy in Detroit schools.

35 **"You can't take part in our democracy":** Bryce Huffman, "Meet Helen Moore: Detroit education activist and state elector," *Detroit Bridge*, December 11, 2020.

36 **"But no one even asked":** Ibid., Rosenbaum.

36 **none more vigorously than:** Jennifer Chambers, "Court Weighs Detroit Literacy Battle," *Detroit News,* October 22, 2019.

37 **questioned whether the money would be spent wisely:** Peter Schmidt, "Detroit Voters Back Unprecedented $1.5 Billion Bond Issue," *EdWeek,* November 16, 1994, https://www.edweek.org/education/detroit-voters-back-unprecedented -1-5-billion-bond-issue/1994/11.

38 **fired all three of the Black firms:** Bill Wylie-Kellermann, "Fifty Years Later. In Detroit the End of Brown: Separate and Unequal," *Radicaldiscipleship,* January 13, 2015, https://radicaldiscipleship.net/2015/01/13/fifty-years-later-in -detroit-the-end-of-brown-separate-and-unequal/.

40 **lawmakers in Lansing threw it out:** Ryan Felton, "Michigan Governor Faces Yet Another Lawsuit—This Time over Detroit Schools," *The Guardian,* April 7, 2016.

40 **"This has nothing to do with our finances":** Ibid, Rosenbaum.

42 **"So, we're still here":** Huffman, "Meet Helen Moore."

CHAPTER 2: THE ROAD TO SEGREGATION

45 **Continental Congress commissioned Koquethagechton:** Eric Sterner, "Conflict and War," *Journal of the American Revolution,* December 18, 2018, https://allthingsliberty.com/2018/12/the-treaty-of-fort-pitt-1778-the-first-u-s -american-indian-treaty/.

47 **"your well known Goodness":** Founders Archives, "Letter to George Washington from George Morgan White Eyes," June 2, 1789, https://founders.archives .gov/documents/Washington/05-02-02-0318.

50 **"appropriately civilized":** James D. Anderson, *The Education of Blacks in the South, 1860–1935* (Chapel Hill: University of North Carolina Press, 1988), 33–47.

51 **a "degraded" people:** Ibid., 38.

52 **"known as the 'Hampton method'"**: Donal F. Lindsey, *Indians at Hampton Institute, 1877–1923* (Urbana: University of Illinois Press, 1995), 112.

53 **"the reason I resigned"**: Ibid.

55 **completely shut out**: Donald P. Baker, "Closed," *Washington Post*, March 4, 2001.

56 **withholding funding from integrated schools**: NAACP Legal Defense Fund, "Southern Manifesto," https://www.naacpldf.org/brown-vs-board/southern -manifesto-massive-resistance-brown/.

57 **white-only segregation academies**: "Coffey v. State Educational Finance Commission, 296 F. Supp. 1389," 1969, https://law.justia.com/cases/federal/district -courts/FSupp/296/1389/1982533/.

57 **remained segregated**: "Private Schools: The Last Refuge," *Time*, November 14, 1969, https://content.time.com/time/subscriber/article/0,33009,840365,00 .html.

57 **remained closed until 1964**: Tony Badger, "Southerners Who Refused to Sign the Southern Manifesto," *Historical Journal* 42, no. 2 (1999): 524.

57 **no great rush**: Baker, "Closed."

60 **"fulfill the constitutional objective"**: Ibid.

60 **"and Prince Edward County"**: Ibid.

62 **personally responsible for repaying the funds to the county**: Charles M. Payne, "'The Whole United States Is Southern!': *Brown v. Board* and the Mystification of Race," *Journal of American History* 91, no. 1 (June 2004); 83–91, https://doi.org/10.2307/3659615; "Closed."

62 **"My country called me to fight in Vietnam"**: "Closed."

64 **most segregated in the nation**: Eliza Shapiro, "Segregation Has Been the Story of New York City's Schools for 50 Years," *New York Times*, March 26, 2019.

65 **not confined to the South**: Matthew F. Delmont, *Why Busing Failed: Race, Media, and the National Resistance to School Desegregation* (Berkeley: University of California Press, 2016), Kindle location 482–86.

65 **significant national consequences**: Fred M. Hechinger, "Big Cities' Protest Demonstrations Threaten New Integration Rift," *New York Times*, February 2, 1964.

66 **"even more unfavorable"**: Ibid.

68 **white families did not want them**: Alana Semuels, "The Utter Inadequacy of

America's Efforts to Desegregate Schools," *The Atlantic,* April 19, 2011, https://www.theatlantic.com/education/archive/2019/04/boston-metco-program-school-desegregation/584224/.

69 **"outrun desegregation":** Alex McLenon, "The 1974 Supreme Court Ruling on Detroit School Busing That Worsened Segregation," WDET Radio, November 19, 2019, https://reganlaw.net/the-u-s-supreme-court-school-busing-ruling-of-forty-years-ago-continues-to-affect-detroit-schools-today/.

70 **the report read:** United States Kerner Commission, *Report of the National Advisory Commission on Civil Disorders* (Washington: United States Kerner Commission, 1968), 65–71.

70 **mass migration from cities:** Othering & Belonging Institute, "Most to Least Segregated," https://belonging.berkeley.edu/most-least-segregated-cities.

71 **preventing further violence:** Ibid., Kerner Commission.

72 **"They're all Southern!":** Kluger, *Simple Justice,* 534.

CHAPTER 3: BLACK TEACHERS MATTER

74 **more bodies remained:** Paul Guzzo, "Clearwater might also have a lost African American cemetery," *Tampa Bay Times,* November 18, 2019.

77 **Between 1939 and 1947:** Kansas Historical Society, "African American Teachers in Kansas," May 2004, https://www.kshs.org/kansapedia/african-american-teachers-in-kansas/11995.

79 **parts of a necessary whole:** Noliwe Rooks, *A Passionate Mind in Relentless Pursuit: The Vision of Mary Mcleoud Bethune* (New York: Penguin Press, 2024), 112.

79 **$2.2 billion today:** Leslie Fenwick, *Jim Crow's Pink Slip: The Untold Story of Black Principal and Teacher Leadership* (Cambridge, Mass.: Harvard Education Press, 2022), 138, https://www.researchgate.net/publication/288421083_The_hardest_deal_of_all_The_battle_over_school_integration_in_Mississippi_1870-1980.

80 **the principal at the school:** Denise Watson, "Barbara Johns Day Honors Student Whose Walkout Contributed to Landmark Desegregation Case," *Virginian Pilot,* April 22, 2018.

81 **add it to his documentation:** Letter from Milton Rooks to Moore about lynch-

ing, Box 2, Folder 17, 1946, https://www.si.edu/media/NMAAHC/NMAAHC
-A2018_12_FindingAid.pdf.

83 **"Yours for Democracy in Florida":** Harry T. Moore, "Voters League Objects to
Senate Literacy Test," *Florida Sentinel,* May 24, 1947.

84 **The Progressive Voters League:** Jake C. Miller, "Harry T. Moore's Campaign
for Racial Equality," *Journal of Black Studies* 31, no. 2 (2000): 214–31, http://
www.jstor.org/stable/2645914.

86 **"must not mean Negro annihilation":** Vanessa Siddle Walker, *The Lost Education of Horace Tate: Uncovering the Hidden Heroes Who Fought for Justice in
Schools* (New York: The New Press, 2018), 3–5.

87 **"the teachers were afraid of them":** *"Behind the Veil,"* Celestine Porter interview recording, August 2, 1995, https://repository.duke.edu/dc/behindtheveil
/btvct08070.

87 **even one Black teacher:** Seth Gerhsonson, Cassandra M. D. Hart, Joshua
Hyman, Constance Lindsay, and Nicholas W. Papageorge, "The Long-Run
Impacts of Same-Race Teachers," National Bureau of Economic Research,
November 2018, https://www.nber.org/papers/w25254.

88 **"Topeka will not want to employ Negro teachers for White children":** "African American Teachers," Kansas Historical Society (n.d.), https://www.kshs.org
/kansapedia/african-american-teachers-in-kansas/11995.

88 **"Shoot the race-mixing invaders!":** James Anthony Schnur, "Desegregation
of Public Schools in Pinellas County, Florida," Digital Commons @ University
of South Florida, 1991, https://digitalcommons.usf.edu/cgi/viewcontent.cgi
?article=4002&context=fac_publications.

89 **the actual source of the problem: the NAACP:** Malcolm Gladwell, "Miss
Buchanan's Period of Adjustment," *Revisionist History,* Season 2, Episode 3,
June 28, 2017, podcast, https://www.simonsaysai.com/blog/miss-buchanans
-period-of-adjustment-revisionist-history-podcast-transcript-b4c65731f73c.

90 **listed the financial support they collected:** Brian J. Daugherity and Charles C.
Bolton, *With All Deliberate Speed: Implementing Brown v. Board of Education*
(Fayetteville: University of Arkansas Press, 2008).

91 **"national directive" to participate in integration lawsuits:** Ibid.

92 **"a sane, unhysterical approach":** Ibid.

92 **assigned to schools with members of their own race:** Ibid.; https://
digitalcommons.usf.edu/cgi/viewcontent.cgi?article=4002&context=fac
_publications.

93 **"separate but really equal":** *With All Deliberate Speed.*

95 **accredited by the Southern Association of Colleges:** Peggy Peterman, "The
Good Old Days Were at Gibbs," *Tampa Bay Times,* May 30, 1993.

95 **after completing her course of study at Gibbs:** Ibid.

95 **School Assignment Committee's gradualist approach:** *With All Deliberate
Speed.*

97 **Fifth Circuit Court demanded all:** Ibid.

97 **James Sanderlin's motion was affirmed:** Ibid.

98 **almost 4,200 new students matriculated:** Ibid.

CHAPTER 4: "WE, TOO, HAD GREAT EXPECTATIONS. AND THEN WE WENT TO SCHOOL."

105 **published their findings in the summer of 1956:** Jason Morgan Ward, "The
D.C. School Hearings of 1956 and the National Vision of Massive Resistance," *Journal of Civil and Human Rights* 1, no. 1 (2015): 82–110, https://doi
.org/10.5406/jcivihumarigh.1.1.0082. See also, Erwin Knoll, "Desegregation's
Tortuous Course," *Commentary,* March 1959, https://www.commentary.org
/articles/erwin-knoll/desegregations-tortuous-course-washington-showcase-of
-integration/.

106 **Governor J. Lindsay Almond Jr. went on television:** Ibid.

107 **"if other actions fail this must be resorted to":** Michael Kohler, "After Bol-
ling: School Desegregation in DC," *Boundary Stones,* March 3, 2021, https://
boundarystones.weta.org/2021/03/03/after-bolling-school-desegregation-dc
#footnote-12.

109 **daily lunches for almost seven thousand hungry children in elementary
schools:** Ibid.

110 **if Black people did not fix their family structures:** Lyndon B. Johnson,
"Remarks on Project Head Start," *Presidency Project,* May 18, 1965, https://www
.presidency.ucsb.edu/documents/remarks-project-head-start.

111   **family background . . . was the biggest determinant:** Elizabeth Evitts Dickinson, "Coleman Report Set the Standard for the Study of Public Education," *Johns Hopkins Magazine,* Winter 2016. https://hub.jhu.edu/magazine/2016/winter/coleman-report-public-education/.

111   **"Good luck, because it's not in my hands":** Ibid.

112   **Coleman's report paved the way:** Leah N. Gordon, "If Opportunity Is Not Enough: Coleman and His Critics in the Era of Equality of Results," *History of Education Quarterly* 57, no. 4 (2017): 601–15, doi:10.1017/heq.2017.35.

112   **"Spent wisely, it helps":** Robert Reinhold, "Texas Ruling: Old System on Trial," New York Times, December 25, 1971.

113   **Coleman later speculated:** Heather C. Hill, "50 Years Ago, One Report Introduced Americans to the Black-White Achievement Gap. Here's What We've Learned Since," *Chalkbeat,* July 13, 2013, https://www.chalkbeat.org/2016/7/13/21103280/50-years-ago-one-report-introduced-americans-to-the-black-white-achievement-gap-here-s-what-we-ve-le.

113   **"Coleman's analysis was not only wrong":** Ibid.

115   **lacked attention to basic rules of pedagogy:** Christine Sleeter, "Why Is There Learning Disabilities? A Critical Analysis of the Birth of the Field in Its Social Context," *Disability Studies Quarterly* 30, no. 2 (2010), https://dsq-sds.org/article/view/1261/1292.

118   **"I saw it on Jim Jeffers":** Rose Mukerji, "A National Demonstration Project Utilizing Televised Materials for the Formal Education of Culturally Disadvantaged Preschool Children," August 1966, https://files.eric.ed.gov/fulltext/ED010529.pdf.

118   **after going shopping on the show:** Ibid.

119   **a basement workshop with ample workspace:** Ibid.

120   **as she thought she might do with *Sesame Street:*** Robert W. Morrow, *Sesame Street and the Reform of Children's Television* (Baltimore: Johns Hopkins University Press, 2006), 52–53.

121   **a group put together by Pierce:** Conrad Lochner, "Dr. Chester Pierce and the 'Hidden Curriculum' of Sesame Street," Joan Ganz Center, February 21, 2021, https://joanganzcooneycenter.org/2021/02/22/dr-chester-pierce/.

122   **agreed to serve as a senior adviser on *Sesame Street:*** Anne Harrington, "Psy-

chiatry, Racism, and the Birth of 'Sesame Street,'" *Bunk History,* May 17, 2019, https://www.bunkhistory.org/resources/psychiatry-racism-and-the-birth-of -sesame-street.

122 **also a doctoral student at UMass Amherst:** Loretta Long, "Sesame Street: A Space Age Approach to Education for Space Age Children" (Ed.D., University of Massachusetts Amherst, 1973), https://doi.org/10.7275/9rcq-5w55.

122 **louder were the calls for law and order:** Timothy J. Lombardo, "When Philadelphia's Foul-Mouthed Cop-Turned-Mayor Invented White Identity Politics," Zocalo Public Square, September 26, 2019, https://www.zocalopublicsquare.org /2019/09/26/when-philadelphias-foul-mouthed-cop-turned-mayor-invented -white-identity-politics/ideas/essay/.

124 **community protests aimed at forcing Girard:** Timothy J. Lombardo, "Civil Rights and the Rise of Frank Rizzo in 1960s Philadelphia," *Pennsylvania Legacies* 18, no. 2 (Fall 2018), https://hsp.org/blogs/fondly-pennsylvania/civil-rights -and-rise-frank-rizzo-1960s-philadelphia.

124 **They were middle and high school students peacefully protesting:** Ibid.

125 **more than three thousand protesters had assembled:** Ibid.

126 **He led the charge into the crowd himself:** Ibid.

128 **mistakenly "treat Black children like the average white child":** Southern Poverty Law Center, "Arthur Jensen," https://www.splcenter.org/fighting-hate /extremist-files/individual/arthur-jensen.

129 **"middle-class environment in a slum neighborhood school":** Elizabeth Kai Hinton, *From the War on Poverty to the War on Crime: The Making of Mass Incarceration in America* (Cambridge, Mass.: Harvard University Press, 2016), 152.

129 **these studies represented a "sophisticated type of backlash":** Edmonds, Ronald, Andrew Billingsley, James Comer, James Dyer, William Hall, Robert Hill, Nan McGehee, Lawrence Reddick, Howard Taylor, and Stephen Wright, "A Black Response to Christopher Jencks's Inequality and Certain Other Issues," *Harvard Educational Review* 43, no.1 (1973): 76–91.

129 **based on the constitutional "equity rights of human beings":** M. A. Farber, "Lawyers' Group Fears an Overreliance on Educational Studies," *New York Times,* June 11, 1972.

CHAPTER 5: UNDEREDUCATED AND OVERPOLICED

136 **Black families had to find the money to pay:** Ibid.

137 **in 1872, when Black leaders decided to pursue a test case:** Rudolph Lapp, *Afro-Americans in California* (San Francisco: Boyd & Fraser Pub. Co., 1979), 18–21.

138 **President Roosevelt defused the situation:** Greg Lucas, "Segregation of Japanese School Kids in San Francisco Sparks an International Incident," California State Library, https://cal170.library.ca.gov/japanese-segregation/.

139 **The courts began to force change:** "A History of Black Americans."

140 **fought for access to neighborhood schools that their children could walk to:** Ibid.

140 **desegregation in San Francisco would function as a one-way system:** Ibid.

141 **Black families and children were to be blamed:** Dan Baum, *Smoke and Mirrors: The War on Drugs and the Politics of Failure* (Seattle: Back Bay Books, 1997), 18.

142 **White parents who had moved out of cities:** Noliwe Rooks, *Cutting School: Privatization, Segregation, and the End of Public Education* (New York: New Press, 2017).

143 **It was a compromise that responded to white fears:** Ibid.

144 **"If you whites can't stop this thing, we Chinese will stop it":** Douglas E. Kneeland, "San Francisco's Chinese Resist School Busing," *New York Times,* September 1, 1971.

145 **he was ill-equipped to lead:** Hill Legal Defense, "Know Your Rights, Wrong Man," *Digital SF,* https://digitalsf.org/islandora/object/islandora%3A113772/datastream/OBJ/view.

145 **They warned the superintendent:** Ibid.

145 **children who were behind academically and needed attention:** Shervon Hunter, "history of Potrero Hill Middle School.1971," YouTube Video, 1:24. *December 21, 2015,* https://www.youtube.com/watch?v=um2TujVi8x0.

146 **it was crucial to learn how to fight:** Hill Legal Defense, "Know Your Rights, Wrong Man."

147 **they said there needed to be more respect:** Ibid.

148 **proposed various techniques to further increase surveillance:** Elizabeth Kai Hinton, *From the War on Poverty to the War on Crime: The Making of*

Mass Incarceration in America (Cambridge, Mass.: Harvard University Press, 2016), 236.

148 **Congresswoman Shirley Chisholm, made her colleagues aware of the connections:** William K. Stevens, "Nixon School Report a Challenge: It Denies Direct Link Between Funds and Pupils' Progress." *New York Times,* March 6, 1970.

150 **"when education could not be entirely withheld it could certainly be made substandard":** Lorraine Hansberry, "The Scars of the Ghetto," *Monthly Review* 67, no. 1 (May 2015).

151 **"deliberately cheated out of one's birthright":** Ibid.

152 **special commendation for educational excellence:** Tammerlin Drummond, "Black Panther School a Legend in Its Time," *East Bay Times,* October 6, 2016.

152 **Huggins's curriculum was innovative:** Ibid.

153 **in 1980, President Ronald Reagan courted her to become secretary of education:** "Marva Collins," National Visionary Leadership Project interviews and conference collection (AFC 2004/007), Archive of Folk Culture, American Folklife Center, Library of Congress, Washington, D.C., https://lccn.loc.gov /2004695153.

153 **started out with only six students:** Marva Collins and Civia Tamarkin, *Marva Collins' Way: Returning to Excellence in Education* (New York: Penguin, 1982), 80.

153 **she used the Socratic method:** Marva Collins Interviews, Library of Congress, *National Visionary Leadership Project.*

153 **"great classics because they expose you to complex thought":** Mikel Kweku Osei Holt, "Marva Collins, The Mother of Black Academic Excellence," *Milwaukee Community Journal,* July 10, 2015.

CHAPTER 6: JELANI

160 **"the most power and the loudest voices":** Kathleen Vail, "Loudest Voices and Unequal Opportunities in the Suburbs," *Kappan,* January 30, 2023, https:// kappanonline.org/interview-with-john-b-diamond-suburban-segregation/.

162 **claims of unequal treatment in schools:** Matthew Hersh, "Police, Parents Clash Over Recent Arrests," *Town Topics,* September 27, 2006.

162 **Princeton also had an important role in ending enforced separation:** Samuel

Freedman, "The Achievement Gap in Elite Schools," *New York Times,* September 28, 2005.

163 **"Princeton was Jim Crow":** Paul Robeson, *Here I Stand* (New York: Othello Associates, 1958), 10.

164 **recruiting more Black teachers:** Vicki Hyman, "When Princeton Attacked Jim Crow," NJ.com, February 8, 2008, https://www.nj.com/ledgerarchives/2008/02/when_princeton_attacked_jim_cr.html.

166 **assist the superintendent of the Trenton public schools:** Jennifer Greenstein Altman, "Unique Princeton Partnership Gives Boost to Trenton Pupils," Princeton University, March 28, 2011, https://www.princeton.edu/news/2011/03/28/unique-princeton-partnership-gives-boost-trenton-pupils.

167 **"what's keeping others from solving it":** Ibid.

168 **When a news crew visited Central High School in Trenton:** David Cantor, "In the Shadow of New Jersey's State Capital, Trenton's Forgotten Schools Struggle to Get Better on Their Own," *The 74 Million,* January 28, 2018: https://www.the74million.org/article/in-the-shadow-of-new-jerseys-state-capital-trentons-forgotten-schools/.

169 **three of the thirty worst-rated were in Trenton:** Erin Vogt, "The 30 worst rated schools in NJ," New Jersey 101.5, 2021-2022, https://nj1015.com/worst-rated-nj-schools/.

CHAPTER 7: COLLEGE ACCESS AND COMMUNITY SCHOOLS

177 **what was required to bring about racial equity:** "Ralph Bunche: An American Odyssey," PBS, https://www.pbs.org/ralphbunche/activist_dilemma.html.

178 **exposure of the average Black student to white people is less today than it was in 1940:** Richard Rothstein, "Racial Segregation Continues and Even Intensifies," *Economic Policy Institute,* February 3, 2012, https://www.epi.org/publication/racial-segregation-continues-intensifies/.

178 **would have reduced medical care expenditures paid by the federal government by nearly $230 billion:** Guangui Wang et al., "School Racial Segregation and the Health of Black Children," *Pediatrics* 149, no. 5 (2022): e2021055952, doi:10.1542/peds.2021-055952.

179 **Black college and university enrollment has been dropping steadily:** "Enroll-

ment Estimates," *National Student Research Center,* May 24, 2023, https://nscresearchcenter.org/current-term-enrollment-estimates/.

181 **twenty-first-century version of separate but equal schools:** Ida Mojadad, "Black Panthers Ran a First-of-Its-Kind Oakland School. Now It's a Beacon for Schools in California," *San Francisco Standard,* August 23, 2023.

182 **today's educational experiment might not last either:** Ibid.

182 **"they will struggle for sustainability":** Ibid.

183 **transforming into hubs that facilitate community-wide collaboration:** David G. Sciarra and Molly A. Hunter, "Resource Accountability: Enforcing State Responsibilities for Sufficient and Equitable Resources Used Effectively to Provide All Students a Quality Education," *Education Policy Analysis Archives* 23 (2015): 21, https://doi.org/10.14507/epaa.v23.2032.

184 **at risk of not even graduating from elementary school:** Erica Green, "LeBron James Opened a School That Was Considered an Experiment. It's Showing Promise," *New York Times,* April 12, 2019.

184 **an additional hour of after-school programming and tutors:** Jessica Poiner, "An In-Depth Analysis of the I Promise's Schools Troubling Academic Results," Fordham Institute, August 7, 2023, https://fordhaminstitute.org/ohio/commentary/depth-analysis-i-promise-schools-troubling-academic-results.

185 **a hole for ourselves that is daunting to contemplate filling:** Poiner, "An In-Depth Analysis."

186 **just the types of neighborhoods and children most in need of impactful, well-rounded schools and caring teachers:** James M. McPartland, "Organizing Schools for Improvement: Lessons from Chicago," *Contemporary Sociology* 40, no. 1 (January 2011): 16–17.

191 **sometimes transformative, sometimes emotionally devastating:** Kevin Mahnken, "Exposure to Desegregated Schools Often Made Whites Less Tolerant as Adults," *The 74 Million,* January 12, 2021, https://www.the74million.org/exposure-to-desegregated-schools-often-made-whites-less-tolerant-as-adults/.

INDEX

social science, 22, 75, 87, 110–11, 113–15, 128, 129, 134
Southern Association of Colleges and Schools, 95
Southern Poverty Law Center, 128
Southern School News, 88
Stanford Center for Education Policy Analysis, 150
Stockton, CA, 136–37
Student Nonviolent Coordinating Committee (SNCC), 124
Students for a Democratic Society, 126
suburbs, 18, 66, 67, 69, 108, 113
white flight to, 63, 70, 140, 142, 149
Sullivan, Neil, 61, 62
Supreme Court, U.S., 13, 61, 63, 68, 77, 83, 85
affirmative action banned by, 11, 186
Brown v. Board of Education, see Brown v. Board of Education
Milliken v. Bradley, 68–69
Plessy v. Ferguson, 53–54, 91, 93, 137
Swann v. Charlotte-Mecklenburg, 97
Swann v. Charlotte-Mecklenburg, 97
Swett, John, 136

Taming the River (Charles et al.), 179
Tampa Bay Times, 94
Taylor, Robert, 59
Teach for America (TFA), 170
Teal, Effie, 95
television programs
as negative influence on Black children, 121–22

Roundabout, 21, 22, 114–20, 122, 124, 130, 131, 147
Sesame Street, 21, 114, 117, 120–22, 147
Terry, Carlton, 59
test scores, 35, 38, 40, 87, 108, 111, 157, 160–61, 168
Thirteenth Annual Report, 136
Thomas, Ernest, 84
Thurmond, Strom, 56
Till, Emmett, 12–13, 21
Titusville Colored Junior High School, 81
Tomlinson Vocational School, 95
Topeka, KS, 5–9, 87–88
Treasure Island military base, 140, 147
Trenton, NJ, 32, 165–72, 175, 178
Trenton Central High School, 168
Tribe, Laurence, 10–11
Ture, Kwame (Stokely Carmichael), 30, 31, 124
Turner, Nat, 52
Tuskegee Institute, 52

United Residents of Pinellas (URP), 97–98
universities, *see* colleges and universities
University of Akron, 183
University of Alabama, 72, 142
University of Chicago, 186
University of Florida, 90, 92
University of Pennsylvania, 179
urban uprisings, 70–71, 123

Vietnam War, 62
Villarreal, Linda, 182, 185

Noliwe Rooks is the L. Herbert Ballou University Professor of Africana Studies and the chair of Africana Studies at Brown University. Her work explores how race and gender both impact and are impacted by popular culture, social history, and political life in the United States. She is the author of five books and is a regular contributor to outlets such as *The New York Times, The Washington Post, The Chronicle of Higher Education, Time,* and NPR.

A NOTE ON THE TYPE

This book was set in Adobe Garamond. Designed for the Adobe Corporation by Robert Slimbach, the fonts are based on types first cut by Claude Garamond (ca. 1480–1561). Garamond was a pupil of Geoffroy Tory and is believed to have followed the Venetian models, although he introduced a number of important differences, and it is to him that we owe the letter we now know as "old style." He gave to his letters a certain elegance and feeling of movement that won their creator an immediate reputation and the patronage of Francis I of France.

Typeset by Scribe,
Philadelphia, Pennsylvania

Designed by Casey Hampton